CAJUN COOKING

Succulent Recipes From Louisiana

CAJUN COOKING

Succulent Recipes From Louisiana

MARJIE LAMBERT

TED SMART

TO TERRY
*who offered me diamonds, adventure
and inspiration*

A QUINTET BOOK

This edition produced by
The Book People Ltd,
Guardian House, Borough Road,
Godalming, Surrey GU7 2AE

Reprinted 1995

ISBN 1-85613-290-0

This book was designed and produced by
Quintet Publishing Limited
6 Blundell Street,
London N7 9BH

Creative Director: Terry Jeavons
Designer: Start Walden
Project Editor: Judith Simons
Editor: Susie Ward
Food Photographer: Trevor Wood
Home Economist: Judith Kelsey
Assisted by: Jonathan Higgins

Typeset in Great Britain by
Central Southern Typesetters, Eastbourne
Manufactured in Singapore by Eray Scan Pte Ltd
Printed in Singapore by
Star Standard Industries private Ltd

AUTHOR'S ACKNOWLEDGEMENTS
With special thanks to my dad, who taught me
not to be afraid of experimenting, and Elaine
Corn, who helped me turn my experiments into
recipes. Thanks also to Judith and Lindsay at
Quintet and to Bob Townsend and Zoe
Zahner at Dingus McGees's.

PICTURE CREDITS

The Publishers would like to thank the following for the
supply of additional photographic material used in this
book.

Key: *t* = top; *b* = bottom; *l* = left; *r* = right.

Michael Freeman: pages 9, 11, 66 *tl tr bl,* 67, 109.

Louisiana Office of Tourism: pages 6, 7, 10, 12, 22, 27, 34,
42, 44, 50, 66 *br,* 84 *l r,* 88, 106.

CONTENTS

INTRODUCTION

——— ★ ———

Louisiana cooking is a great conglomeration of influences from the many ethnic groups that have populated the state for more than 200 years. Yet, each ingredient in that melting pot is distinct and can be traced to its roots.

In Louisiana, and especially in New Orleans, life frequently revolves around food and discussions of food. There is a great love of eating and cooking that predated and has outlasted America's brief 1980s' love affair with celebrity chefs and the chic restaurant of the moment. Many of New Orleans' best restaurants are known far beyond Louisiana and have been operating for several decades, exceptions in an industry known for short-lived ventures.

It is a telling piece of evidence that when Cajuns trace their history from Nova Scotia to Louisiana, it is intertwined with a story about food. It goes like this:

In 1755, when British soldiers drove a colony of French settlers out of Nova Scotia and their colony of Acadia for refusing to swear allegiance to Britain, the lobster went with the Acadians, according to the legend. The Acadians and the lobster, the legend continues, wandered for years through Canada and the east coast colonies of what would become the United States, until they reached Louisiana, colonized by the French nearly a century earlier. Finding kinship there, and swampy land that no one else wanted, the Acadians settled along the waterways of southern Louisiana, south and west of New Orleans. The name Acadians, through years of mispronounciation, was eventually shortened to Cajuns. And the lobster, worn down to a tiny creature by the long, hard trip, settled into the bayous and became the crawfish.

The crawfish – or freshwater crayfish – Louisiana's most valuable commercial catch, is still one of the Cajun's best friends. It is a staple – and often the unofficial logo – of Cajun cooking, a style of cuisine that is based on the country cooking of his French ancestors, but has evolved around local ingredients and possesses its own distinctive style. Gumbo uses many of the same ingredients as French bouillabaisse, for example, but the Cajun methods of preparation disguise those bloodlines.

The staple ingredients of Cajun cooking were what people could hunt, catch, or grow. From the bayous, they pulled crawfish, alligators, frogs, and many species of fish. The coastal marshes were – and still are – a midway stopping point for ducks and other game birds that migrate between Canada and South America, and a winter home for others. From the Gulf of Mexico, the Cajuns caught prawns, oysters and more fish. They had large home gardens – especially sweet potatoes, Creole tomatoes, squashes, aubergines and, of course, okra – in the rich soil and subtropical climate, and raised chicken and pigs.

Creole cuisine is the more sophisticated city cousin of Cajun cooking. It also has French roots, but has been more influenced by the cooking of other ethnic groups. Louisiana, a French crown colony in the early 1700s, was ceded to Spain, then went back to French control before the United States bought it in the great Louisiana Purchase of 1803. There were large immigrations of Germans, Italians and Hungarians, while the slave trade brought thousands of Africans. Local Indians also contributed to the cuisine. New Orleans, being a port city, was a center for trade with the West Indies, Cuba and Mexico. Where Cajun cooking is hearty and rustic country fare, Creole-style food is more aristocratic. But in many cases, the line between the two cuisines has been blurred or even erased.

In addition to local ingredients, Louisiana cuisine is typified by thick and complex sauces, the use of roux and freshly-made stocks, and long cooking times. Seasoning is critical as well. Louisiana cooks say their dishes should have a flavour to set each taste bud off and keep it dancing. Most Cajun food is very spicy – it sometimes seems that you should just dump the entire contents of your spice rack into some dishes, but in reality the flavours are carefully chosen to complement each other and fill the mouth with sensation. Many are also hot with cayenne and other peppers. A large number of recipes begin with the Holy Trinity of Louisiana cooking: that is, chopped onions, bell peppers and celery.

Although Cajuns have been in southern Louisiana for more than two centuries, it was many years before their cooking began to spread beyond the bayous of what they called new Acadiana. Physically, the Cajuns remained fairly isolated until the mid 1970s, when the construction of an interstate highway across the wilderness of the Atchafalaya

OPPOSITE Lafayette is the cultural heart of Acadiana. It boasts the Acadian Village, an historical re-creation of a Cajun community of the 1800s. Every spring, Lafayette celebrates the Azalea Trail, pictured here.

ABOVE Avery Island lies near New Iberia, deep in Cajun country. Its 300 acres are a horticultural paradise, thick with camellias, irises, azaleas and tropical plants, and a bird sanctuary where egrets nest.

Basin created a shortcut between New Orleans and the heart of Cajun country. A few years later, Cajun cooking styles began to spread beyond New Orleans, and soon, the Cajun craze swept the United States.

For many people, their introduction to Cajun cooking was blackened redfish, a highly-spiced fish fillet cooked very quickly at a very high temperature. Although not a traditional Cajun dish, it was an instant classic, and with good reason. But to many people, ignorant of a culinary history more than 200 years old, blackened redfish became the symbol of Cajun cooking. The demand created a shortage of redfish so severe that the state of Louisiana imposed a temporary ban on the sale of redfish caught in the Gulf of Mexico off Louisiana. Outside Louisiana, many people overlooked the gumbos, the jambalayas, the étouffées, and the crawfish – its history part of Cajun lore – and erroneously defined Cajun cooking as anything blackened or anything seasoned with cayenne.

When Cajun fever subsided, and cooks stopped blackening everything from oysters to aubergines, it was clear that the recipes and ingredients of rural southern Louisiana cooks had influenced menus everywhere. Catfish became respectable. Andouille sausage, a spicy Cajun sausage of smoked pork, gained wide popularity – and imitators. Jambalaya was adopted by many cooks as part of their repertoire. So-called Cajun BBQ Shrimp – actually prawns simmered in a butter sauce made incredibly hot by cayenne and other peppers – is hugely popular.

In some respects, Cajun cooking remains a style of another century. In an era of calorie and cholesterol consciousness, Cajun recipes use huge amounts of fat, butter and cream. There have been some concessions to health concerns, with Commander's Palace restaurant leading the way with lighter sauces, roux-less gumbos and traditional ingredients encased in light soufflés.

This cookbook tries to respond in the same way. It reduces the quantity of roux in many recipes, replaces double cream with single cream, cuts the amount of oil used to sauté vegetables, and grills fish and sautés meat instead of deep-frying it where the taste of a dish is not significantly affected. But it is also true that heavy sauces and creams are integral to a style of cooking with a long history. Eliminate the roux, the cream soups and sauces, and the fried food, and you eliminate the cuisine.

TRADITIONAL CAJUN
INGREDIENTS

— ★ —

It's been said that the swamp floor is the pantry of the Cajun kitchen, and, indeed, the swamp produces one of the staples of the Cajun menu, the crawfish. Some of its other distinctive ingredients, including frogs, alligators and catfish, also come from the swamp. But the Gulf of Mexico gives Louisiana chefs their prawns, oysters and dozens of varieties of fish. The Cajun hunting tradition contributes ducks, rabbits and other game animals. And the history of Cajuns in Louisiana, which dates back more than 200 years, is that of rural country folk relying on their gardens for produce and small farms for chicken and pork.

Many Cajun ingredients are available in this country, though they just are not displayed as prominently or in as great a quantity elsewhere as they are in Bayou country. The variety of crab or oyster in your grocery may be different than the type pulled from the waters of Louisiana, but all varieties work in the recipes in this book.

Widely-used ingredients in Louisiana cooking include rice, which absorbs the rich sauces and tames the hot spices of Cajun dishes; cayenne and other hot peppers that are dried and ground and used for seasoning; Creole mustard, a sharp-tasting brown mustard with whole seeds; corn-flour, a non-wheat flour milled from corn and used to bread items before frying; okra, a green pod vegetable that

ABOVE For more than two centuries, Cajun farmers have sold their luscious fruits and vegetables at the 100-odd produce stalls in the French Market in New Orleans' French Quarter.

is sliced and used to thicken gumbo; filé powder, ground sassafras leaf that is used to season and thicken gumbo; mirliton, a pear-shaped vegetable related to the cucumber and also known as chayote; a wide variety of herbs, including parsley, thyme, oregano and basil; pecans; peaches; auber-gines, spring onions, artichokes, sweet potatoes, red (kidney) beans, Creole tomatoes, and, of course, the Holy Trinity of green peppers, onions and celery. All of the above are available here, except for Creole mustard, filé powder and mirlitons. To approximate the first, use whole seed and English mustard. Both filé powder and mirliton cannot be duplicated, though the latter can sometimes be found in the food hall of London superstores.

CRAWFISH. This creature, affectionately known as a craw-dad or mudbug because of its habit of tunnelling deep into the mud to keep cool, has become a symbol of sorts for Cajun cooking. Although 'crawdads' – freshwater crayfish

OPPOSITE *Paddleboats along the Mississippi River recall the 19th century, the days of Mark Twain and riverboat gamblers.*

RIGHT *Louisiana has miles and miles of rivers and swamps, and canoeing – alone or with a guide – can give a visitor a breathtaking sample of bayou country, including close-up views of alligators.*

– can be found on every continent except Africa, it is only in Cajun cooking that they have such an important part. Ninety percent of the world's commercial crawfish come from Louisiana, and most of those are eaten in Louisiana, although some are shipped around the world, especially to Finland and Sweden. With the growing popularity of Cajun cooking in the last decade, the demand for crawfish has increased to the point where people 'farm' them commercially in ponds, which often double as rice paddies.

Louisiana's Cajun country is dotted with tiny places that serve boiled crawfish whole. They are one of the world's easiest meals: Throw some crab and shrimp into boiling water in a big stockpot, add a sliced lemon and let simmer a few minutes to develop flavour, then add the live or defrosted crawfish. Boil 10 minutes, drain and serve. To eat them, give the tail a quick twist until it snaps off from the rest of the body. Peel a couple of segments from the top of the tail, squeeze the tip, and the tail meat should pop out in one piece. Remove the black vein and eat.

Crawfish are generally available live, boiled whole and frozen, or in the form of tail meat that has been shelled and blanched. If your grocer or fish market does not carry freshwater crayfish, ask if they can specially order it.

One item on the Cajun-Creole menu is the soft-shell crawfish, raised commercially and watched carefully until it sheds its shell. At this point it is plucked from the water and frozen before a new shell can harden. These are only available in a couple of Cajun-style restaurants in the UK.

The yellow-orange 'fat' from the crawfish, actually its liver and pancreas, is considered a delicacy. Much of the wonderful flavour in a crawfish bisque comes from the fat.

CRAB. Blue-claw, soft-shell and buster crabs are the type most commonly used in Louisiana cuisine, but meat from other types of crab – Dungeness, King, Snow, and Stone crabs among others – work well in these recipes. Buying whole crabs is recommended, so the carcass can be used to make a delicious stock, but fresh, frozen and canned crab meat are also acceptable. In some places, crab claws, especially King Crab claws, are sold separately, pre-cooked and ready for dipping.

Soft-shell crabs are not a separate species of crab, but ones that are harvested in the brief period after they shed the shells they have outgrown, but before they grow new ones. These are not found in Britain, so ordinary crab meat must be substituted. Learn how much meat the whole crab available locally produces. While it may take a dozen or more blue crabs to produce one pound of meat, two medium Dungeness crabs will produce the same amount.

OYSTERS. Oysters are used generously in Cajun and Creole cooking. They are key ingredients in soups, gumbos and jambalayas, and are the stars of dishes such as Oysters Bienville (pages 20–21) or Deep-Fried Oysters (page 22). Gulf Oysters and Louisiana Oysters are commonly used in Louisiana cooking, but use whatever fresh oysters are available locally. When buying oysters still in the shell, look for ones that are tightly closed. If you don't eat them right away, cover them with a damp towel but don't water them. Fresh oysters should be plump, have a creamy colour and be surrounded by clear liquid.

To shell an oyster, protect your hand with heavy gloves, a potholder or a towel. Cutting your hand with the sharp edge of an oyster shell is not only painful, but can cause a bad infection. Place the oyster on a flat surface with the deep, rounded side down. Find the hinge, and insert the tip

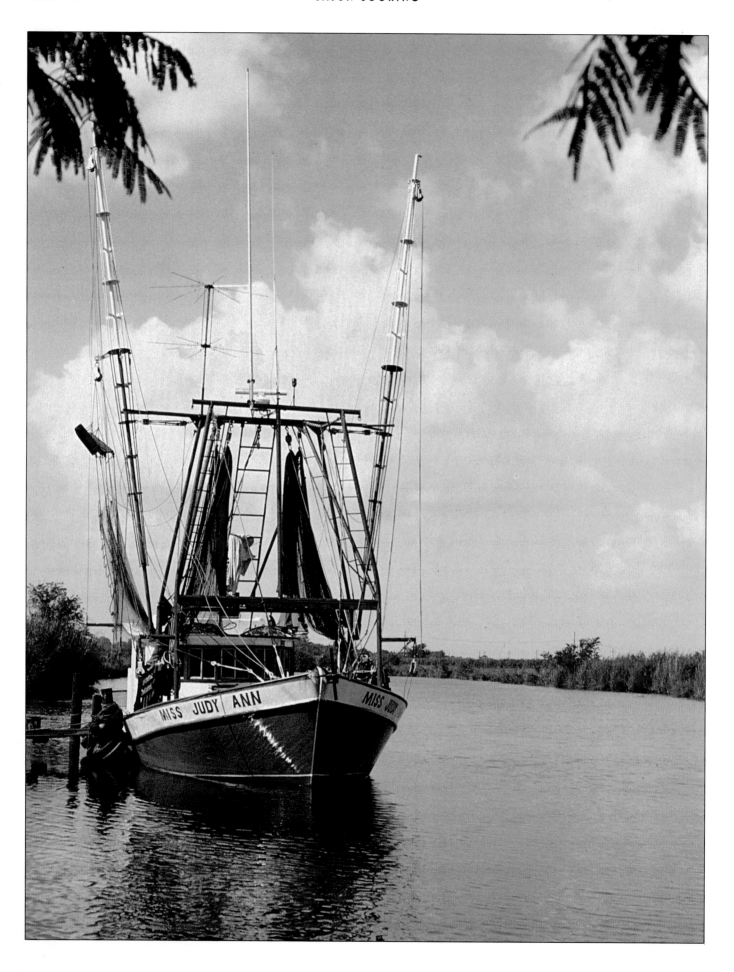

of an oyster knife between the top and bottom shells. Working carefully, pry the two shells slightly apart, then slide the oyster knife or a long slender blade between the oyster and the top shell and sever the muscle that connects them. Carefully remove the top shell so that you don't lose any of the oyster liquor. Slide the knife under the oyster and cut the muscle connecting it to the bottom shell.

Oysters need very little cooking. For many recipes, the heat of a soup or gumbo that has been just removed from the stove is enough to cook the oyster. Cook only until the edges begin to curl. An overcooked oyster can take on the texture of leather.

PRAWNS. Use fresh prawns whenever available. Frozen prawns, which seem to be increasingly what is offered for sale, can become mushy and flavourless. If you can find them, buy prawns with the heads still on. The heads produce no meat but make wonderful stock. Asian markets sometimes stock whole prawns, or ask your fishmonger if whole prawns can be specially ordered. If a recipe calls for one pound of large headless prawns, buy two pounds of whole prawns. The per-pound price of whole prawns is typically about half the price of headless prawns, so the total cost will be about the same. Most stores still sell prawns in the shell, but the demands for convenience are prompting more stores to sell raw prawns already shelled and deveined. Hold out for prawns in the shell when you can. Even if you don't need stock for this recipe, you will probably want the shells to make stock in the next few weeks. Just freeze them until you need them.

To clean whole prawns cut off the tail right behind the head. Remove the legs and open the shell lengthways, gently pulling it off at the end toward the head. You may leave the soft tail fins attached, if desired. To devein – especially in larger prawns, where the vein tends to be gritty – make a shallow cut lengthways down what looks like the back spine. Pull out the vein or wash it free.

FISH. Catfish, redfish, red snapper, speckled trout and pompano are the fish used most in Louisiana cooking, but in most Cajun-Creole recipes, you can substitute pretty freely similar fish that are available locally.

Catfish have become so popular that they are farmed in commercial ponds throughout the United States, although Mississippi is the biggest producer. There are about 20 species of catfish, but channel catfish, a white-fleshed, firm-textured, medium-oily fish, is the most common commercial species. Catfish have a tough, inedible skin that must be removed. Frying catfish is the most popular means of preparation, but it can also be served poached, steamed, baked, grilled or sautéed.

Pompano is a gourmet fish, delicious and very expensive. It lives in the Atlantic Ocean and the Caribbean. It is moderately fatty and firm textured, and does not fry well. It is excellent stuffed with crab and baked whole, or grilled.

Substitute whole rainbow trout or flounder fillets.

Redfish is related to the Atlantic coast drum or croaker and the speckled trout of the Gulf. It became so popular in the 1980s as Cajun blackened redfish that it is now scarce in Gulf waters, and the state of Louisiana has temporarily banned its sale. It is a low-fat, firm-textured fish. As substitutes, try sea bass or brown trout.

Red snapper is widely available along the Gulf and Atlantic coasts. It is a low-fat, firm-textured fish with vivid rose skin. Filleted, red snapper can be substituted for redfish and blackened. It is an adaptable fish that can be cooked a variety of ways. Acceptable substitutes include sea bass and redfish. Orange roughy, a delicately flavoured New Zealand fish works well in snapper recipes, but this too is hard to find here.

Speckled trout has firm, white flesh and a delicate flavour and can be cooked many ways. Its size makes it perfect for single servings. Try it filleted and grilled. Other trout, including rainbow and brown trout, may be substituted, or try sea bass, orange roughy or small plaice.

ANDOUILLE SAUSAGE. This is a spicy Cajun smoked-pork sausage. Some gourmet delicatessens sell it, otherwise your best bet is to go for Polish kielbasa – but since Andouille supplies part of the spicy flavour in some recipes, be sure to adjust the seasonings if you use something else.

TASSO. A very highly seasoned smoked pork or ham, Tasso is rarely used as the star ingredient, but as a flavouring in jambalayas and other dishes. You may substitute another type of smoked ham, but add more cayenne and other seasonings if you want the dish to be spicy.

TABASCO SAUCE. The brand name of a Louisiana hot sauce made on Avery Island, deep in Cajun country. Very hot red peppers are ground with salt, fermented in oak barrels, then pickled with vinegar. Other manufacturers make similar hot-pepper sauces.

OPPOSITE *A shrimp boat weighs anchor on the Louisiana bayou, home to many ingredients of Cajun cooking.*

THE BASICS

——— ★ ———

ROUX

Roux is a crucial ingredient in many Cajun dishes, including gumbo, crawfish étouffée, grillades and crawfish bisque. It is a thickener, but more important, it is a flavouring agent. A dark brown roux adds an incredible richness to a crawfish bisque, for example. Because of today's health concerns, I've reduced the quantity of roux used in some dishes, but left some in the recipes because of the flavour it adds.

≈ Roux is an ingredient to be treated with respect. It should be cooked slowly and must have constant attention. If the flour burns, you'll see black specks in the mixture. At that point, throw it out and start again. Otherwise the scorched taste will permeate the food. If you don't use care, the roux may splatter you. If it does, its high temperature will raise blisters. That's why some call it 'Cajun napalm.'

≈ Roux is traditionally cooked over a low heat, with constant stirring or whisking. Made the traditional way, a dark mahogany roux will take 45 minutes to 1 hour to make. For the impatient, Paul Prudhomme recommends cooking quickly over high heat. But his method is too tricky for cooks unskilled in making roux. Start slowly, and adjust to your own pace. I use medium-low heat, and my dark roux requires about 25 minutes. Even so, the roux must be stirred constantly.

≈ Some people also recommend microwaving roux. I don't like this method as well because it has a greater tendency to become grainy. I have, however, included a recipe for microwave roux here.

≈ Even after you have removed roux from the heat, the high temperature in the fat will continue cooking the flour. The way to stop the cooking process is to stir in some or all of the chopped vegetables called for in the recipe.

≈ I prefer to use lard in my roux, but you may also use vegetable oil.

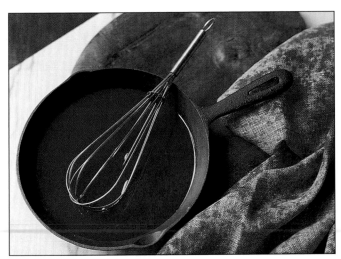

BASIC ROUX

BASIC ROUX:

225 g/8 oz lard
100 g/4 oz plain flour

≈ In a heavy saucepan over medium-low to low heat, melt the lard. When it is hot, add about one-third of the flour at a time, whisking it until smooth each time. Continue stirring after all the flour is added. As the roux cooks, you will see the colour darken and it will develop a nutty smell. Continue cooking until the roux reaches the desired colour. DO NOT STOP STIRRING UNTIL THE ROUX IS DONE.

≈ When the roux reaches the desired colour, remove it from the heat and stir in vegetables to stop the cooking. If no vegetables are called for, pour the roux into a metal bowl and continue stirring for 5-10 minutes until the darkening stops. At this point, you may return the roux and vegetables to the stock and continue the recipe, or set the roux aside and let it cool.

≈ Excess roux may be refrigerated or frozen.

PEANUT-BUTTER-COLORED ROUX   MEDIUM RED-BROWN ROUX   DARK, MAHOGANY-COLORED ROUX

MICROWAVE ROUX

≈ In an oven-tempered, 1.75 l/3 pt glass container, melt the lard. Whisk in the flour. Microwave on high power (100 percent) in 3-minute periods, stirring well after every period. (The glass will be very hot.) Cook until the roux begins to separate and turn brown. Then microwave for 1-minute periods, stirring each time. When the roux reaches the desired colour, stir in the chopped vegetables to stop the cooking, then continue with the recipe. Or, if you do not intend to add vegetables at this point, pour the roux into a bowl and continue stirring for 5-10 minutes.

STOCKS

Stock is the base upon which many Louisiana dishes are built. You can't make gumbos or most soups without it, and it is an important ingredient in various stews, pasta sauces and savoury pie fillings. Sure, you can use tinned broth or clam juice, but the richness of flavour of a long-simmered, homemade stock will be missing from the finished dish.

Making your own stock means you cannot take advantage of some of the convenience of today's meat and seafood products. It's difficult to find raw prawns with heads on, for example, and more stores are catering to working people by offering prawns already shelled, de-veined, cooked and frozen. Yes, it is a lot of work to crack and clean your own crabs, and the task seems especially daunting if you do not need seafood stock to go with that crab. But that carcass will be invaluable next week or the week after. Buying a whole chicken means that you get the back and neck to make stock. Then freeze those shrimp and crab shells, the carcass of last night's roast duck, the neck and back from the chicken, the bones from the rib roast. Save them until you have an afternoon when you can let them simmer for hours on the back burner.

If you know you'll be making stock in a few days, don't throw away the limp carrot, the celery leaves or the nearly naked parsley stems. Save them in a plastic bag for stock.

where the aesthetics of your vegetables are not important, just their flavour.

Some tips:
≈ Green peppers, bloody fish parts and livers give stock a bad taste. Do not use them.
≈ Do not salt your stock. As the stock reduces, the salty flavour will intensify.
≈ Do not add chopped herbs or spices until you're ready to cook with the stock, or you may skim them off when you remove fat or foam. (Obviously, that is not a problem with whole items such as bay leaves, sprigs of fresh herbs, cloves and peppercorns.)
≈ For safety reasons, do not refrigerate stock longer than two days. For reasons of taste, do not freeze it longer than six months.

POULTRY AND GAME STOCK

Use 900 g/2 lb any combination of backs, necks and bones from chickens, ducks, rabbits, geese, etc. Do not use livers. If you have time, roast the bones at 180°C/350°F/Gas Mark 4 for about 40 minutes. This will make a richer stock. You may also add trimmings from any other vegetable – except green peppers – you are using in a particular recipe.

MAKES 900 ML/1½ PTS

1 onion, cut into chunks
1 stalk celery, leaves included, sliced
1 clove garlic, crushed
1 carrot, unpeeled, cut into chunks.
1 sprig fresh parsley
5 whole black peppercorns

≈ Put all ingredients in a large pot. Add 900 ml/1½ pts water. Make a mental note of the water level in the pot, because you need at least 900 ml/1½ pts stock after it has simmered for several hours. Add another 900 ml/1½ pts water, enough to cover the bones and vegetables by several inches. Bring to the boil. Skim off any foam. Reduce heat and simmer for at least 4 hours, adding extra water if necessary to keep at least 900 ml/1½ pts liquid in the pot.
≈ Strain the stock, discarding the bones and vegetables. If you plan to use immediately, skim the fat from the top. Otherwise, cool and refrigerate. Stock should be cooled quickly to avoid spoiling, but should not be put directly from the stove into the refrigerator. Run 5–7.5 cm/2–3 inches of cold water into the sink, and add ice if you want. Pour the stock into small containers. As soon as the stock comes close to room temperature, refrigerate. After several hours, the fat will have congealed on the top and can be removed easily. Freeze or return to the refrigerator.

BROWN MEAT STOCK

Use 900 g/2 lb, any combination, of necks and bones from beef, veal and/or pork. If you have time, roast the bones at 180°C/350°F/Gas Mark 4 until thoroughly browned. This will give stock a richer flavour. You may also add trimmings from any other vegetable – except green peppers – you are using in a particular recipe.

MAKES 900 ML/1½ PTS

1 onion, cut into chunks
1 stalk celery, leaves included, sliced
1 clove garlic, unpeeled, cut into chunks
1 sprig fresh parsley
5 whole black peppercorns

≈ Put all ingredients in a large pot. Add 900 ml/1½ pts water. Make a mental note of the water level in the pot, because you need at least 900 ml/1½ pts stock after it has simmered several hours. Add another 900 ml/1½ pts water, enough to cover the bones and vegetables by several inches. Bring mixture to the boil. Skim off any foam. Reduce heat and simmer for at least 4 hours, adding water if necessary, to keep at least 900 ml/1½ pts liquid in the pot.
≈ Strain the stock, discarding the bones and vegetables. If you plan to use immediately, skin the fat from the top. Otherwise, cool and refrigerate. Stock should be cooled quickly to avoid spoiling, but shouldn't be put directly from the stove into the refrigerator. Run 5–7.5 cm/2–3 inches of cold water into the sink, and add ice if you want. Pour the stock into small containers and place the containers in the sink. As soon as the stock comes near room temp-erature, refrigerate. After it has been in the refrigerator several hours, the fat will have congealed on the top and can be removed easily. Freeze or return to refrigerator.

SEAFOOD STOCK

Use 900 g/2 lb, any combination of prawn shells and heads crab shells, crayfish heads and shells, lobster carcasses and fish carcasses with heads and gills removed. You may also add oyster liquor. You may also add trimmings from any other vegetable – except green peppers – you are using in a particular recipe.

MAKES 900 ML/1½ PTS

1 onion, cut into chunks
1 stalk celery, leaves included, sliced
1 clove garlic, crushed
1 carrot, unpeeled, cut into chunks
1 sprig fresh parsley
5 whole black peppercorns

≈ Put all ingredients in a large pot. Add 900 ml/1½ pts water. Make a mental note of the water level, because you want to have at least 900 ml/1½ pts of stock after it has simmered several hours. Add another 900 ml/1½ pts water, enough to cover the shells and vegetables by several inches. Bring to the boil. Skim off the grey foam. Reduce heat and simmer for at least 4 hours, adding extra water if necessary, to keep at least 900 ml/1½ pts liquid in the pot.

≈ Strain the stock, discarding the shells and vegetables. If you are not using immediately, cool and refrigerate. Stock should be cooled quickly to avoid spoiling, but should not be put directly from the stove into the refrigerator. Run 5–7.5 cm/2–3 inches of cold water into the sink, and add ice if you want. Pour the stock into small containers and place the containers in the sink. As soon as the stock comes close to room temperature, refrigerate or freeze.

APPETIZERS

——★——

OYSTERS ROCKEFELLER

An elegant dish for oyster lovers that combines the mellow tastes of oysters and spinach. Louisiana cooks used to flavour this with absinthe, a licorice-flavoured liqueur that's been outlawed in the United States. I've used aniseed, but you could also substitute Pernod or any other aniseed-flavoured liqueur.

SERVES 4

rock salt
50 g/2 oz butter
225 g/8 oz chopped fresh spinach
45 ml/3 tbsp chopped fresh parsley
6 spring onions, chopped
30 ml/2 tbsp finely chopped celery
15 ml/1 tbsp finely chopped green pepper
1.5 ml/¼ tsp salt
1.5 ml/¼ tsp aniseed
7.5 ml/1½ tsp fresh thyme or 2.5 ml/½ tsp dried
15 ml/1 tbsp anchovy paste
45 ml/3 tbsp dry breadcrumbs
120 ml/4 fl oz double cream
pinch of fresh ground black pepper
few drops of Tabasco sauce
20 oysters on the half shells

OVEN TEMPERATURE: 200°C/400°F/Gas Mark 6

≈ Pour the rock salt about 1.2 cm/½ inch deep into a large baking pan, and put into the oven at 200°C/400°F/Gas Mark 6. The salt serves to keep the oysters from tipping over, and it will help keep them warm after they come out of the oven.

≈ In a frying pan over low heat, melt the butter. Sauté the spinach, parsley, onions, celery and green pepper until the spinach is thoroughly wilted, about 6 minutes. Add remaining ingredients, except the oysters, stirring in a little extra cream or breadcrumbs as needed to achieve the consistency of a thick sauce.

≈ Put 1 oyster on each half shell and spoon some of the sauce over each oyster. Nestle the oysters in the heated rock salt. Bake at 200°C/400°F/Gas Mark 6 until the topping is bubbly, about 12 minutes.

OYSTERS BIENVILLE

Prawns, mushrooms and Parmesan cheese create a delicious topping that is a truly wonderful complement to the delicate oyster taste. This dish is named for Jean Baptiste le Moyne, Sieur de Bienville, founder of New Orleans.

SERVES 3–4

rock salt
25 g/1 oz butter
3 spring onions, minced
2 cloves garlic, minced
1 tbsp finely chopped fresh parsley
4 large mushrooms, finely chopped
15 g/½ oz plain flour
175 ml/6 fl oz double cream
100 g/4 oz prawns, shelled, deveined, cooked and finely chopped
1 egg yolk, lightly beaten
15 ml/1 tbsp dry sherry
large pinch black pepper
large pinch cayenne
5 ml/1 tsp Worcestershire sauce
pinch of salt
75 ml/5 tbsp grated Parmesan cheese
30 ml/2 tbsp dry breadcrumbs
2.5 ml/¼ tsp salt
large pinch cayenne
large pinch black pepper
16 oysters on the half shell

OVEN TEMPERATURE: 200°C/400°F/Gas Mark 6

≈ Pour the rock salt about 1.2 cm/½ inch deep into a large baking tin, or several tins, large enough to hold all the oysters in one layer, and put in oven at 200°C/400°F/Gas Mark 6. The salt keeps the oysters from tipping over, and will help keep them warm after they come out of the oven.

≈ In a frying pan over a moderate heat, melt the butter. Sauté the spring onions, garlic, parsley and mushrooms until the vegetables are limp, about 5 minutes. Add the flour and stir until blended. Add the cream and stir until blended. Add the prawns, egg yolk, sherry, black pepper, cayenne, Worcestershire sauce and salt and cook until the mixture thickens, stirring, 5–6 minutes.

≈ In a small bowl, make the crumb topping mixture. Combine the Parmesan, breadcrumbs, salt, cayenne and pepper.

≈ Put 1 oyster on each half shell and spoon some prawn sauce over each oyster. Top each with the crumb mixture. Nestle the oysters in hot rock salt. Bake at 200°C/400°F/Gas Mark 6 until the topping is golden, 12–15 minutes.

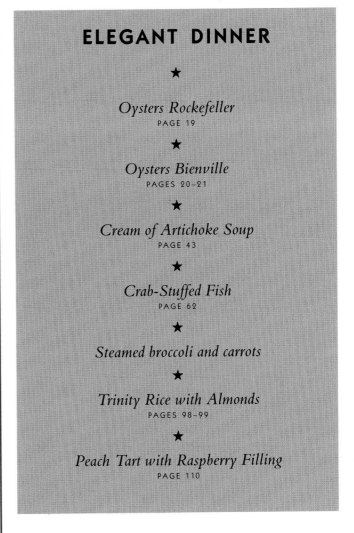

ELEGANT DINNER

★

Oysters Rockefeller
PAGE 19

★

Oysters Bienville
PAGES 20–21

★

Cream of Artichoke Soup
PAGE 43

★

Crab-Stuffed Fish
PAGE 62

★

Steamed broccoli and carrots

★

Trinity Rice with Almonds
PAGES 98–99

★

Peach Tart with Raspberry Filling
PAGE 110

DEEP-FRIED OYSTERS

Even people who don't eat oysters will love these hot, crisp finger foods. Cooked quickly at high heat, the delicate and juicy flavour of the oysters is sealed in. Cornflour can be found in many natural food stores. You may use cornmeal in place of the cornflour, and the result will be a slightly coarser, heavier, but still delicious, coating.

SERVES 4–6

175 g/6 oz cornmeal
90 ml/6 tbsp cornflour
5 ml/1 tsp salt
2.5 ml/½ tsp black pepper
2.5 ml/½ tsp cayenne
2 dozen fresh oysters, shelled
vegetable oil for frying

≈ Combine all the ingredients, except the oysters and oil. Pat the oysters dry with kitchen paper, then dip the oysters in the cornmeal mixture.

≈ In a deep frying pan or wok, heat the oil to 185°C/365°F. With tongs, drop in 4 or 5 oysters at a time and cook until golden brown, turning once and making sure they don't touch, about 3 minutes. Drain well on kitchen paper and keep warm while you fry the remaining oysters. Make sure the oil has returned to 185°C/365°F before cooking each batch. Serve hot with Cocktail Sauce (page 121) for dipping the oysters into.

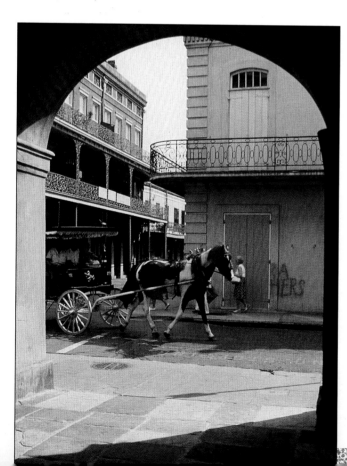

MUSHROOMS WITH PRAWN-CORNBREAD STUFFING

These mushrooms, served hot, make a tasty snack or a first course. You may substitute crayfish tails for the prawns. If you're making Crawfish Bisque (pages 43–45), make some extra stuffing and add spices (the stuffing in the bisque picks up its flavour from the broth), then use it in these mushrooms.

MAKES 24

24 medium to large mushrooms
25 g/1 oz butter
100 g/4 oz chopped onion
4 spring onions, chopped
½ green pepper, chopped
1 stalk celery, chopped
2 cloves garlic, finely chopped
30 ml/2 tbsp chopped fresh parsley
5 ml/1 tsp fresh thyme or 1.5 ml/¼ tsp. dried
2.5 ml/½ tsp salt
1.5 ml/¼ tsp black pepper
1.5 ml/¼ tsp cayenne
2.5 ml/½ tsp dry mustard
5 ml/1 tsp lemon juice
1 egg, lightly beaten
100 g/4 oz finely crumbled cornbread (pages 96–97)
100 g/4 oz small cooked prawns, shelled and coarsely chopped
seafood stock (page 17) or milk to moisten

OVEN TEMPERATURE: 180°C/350°F/Gas Mark 4

≈ Clean the mushrooms and separate the stems from the caps. Discard the stems or save for another use. Steam the mushroom caps for 5 minutes, then set aside.

≈ In medium frying pan, melt the butter over low heat. Sauté the onions, pepper, celery and garlic until limp, about 5 minutes. Put in a medium bowl. Add the remaining ingredients, except the stock or milk, then mix well. Add enough stock or milk so the mixture is thoroughly moistened, but not mushy.

≈ Stuff the mushroom caps with the prawn mixture, mounding a little on each top. Arrange on lightly greased baking sheet. Bake at 180°C/350°F/Gas Mark 4 until stuffing is lightly browned, 10–15 minutes. Serve hot.

LEFT *The French Quarter was the birthplace of New Orleans and still retains the narrow streets that were laid out by the French. Its carefully restored buildings, many of them* more than a century old, are noted for their balconies and intimate courtyards. The French Quarter is alive with jazz clubs, antique shops and world-famous restaurants.

PAN-FRIED OYSTERS

These pan-fried oysters are almost as delicious as deep-fried oysters, but not quite as intimidating for someone who is not adept at deep-frying.

SERVES 3–4

50 g/2 oz plain flour
50 g/2 oz dry breadcrumbs
2.5 ml/½ tsp salt
2.5 ml/½ tsp black pepper
2.5 ml/½ tsp cayenne
1.5 ml/¼ tsp dried thyme
2 eggs, lightly beaten
30 ml/2 tbsp milk
2 dozen fresh oysters, shelled
butter for frying

≈ Combine the flour, breadcrumbs, salt, pepper, cayenne and thyme. In another bowl, combine the eggs and milk.

≈ Pat the oysters dry with kitchen paper. Quickly dip the oysters in the crumb mixture, then in the egg mixture, then again in the crumbs.

≈ In a frying pan, melt 30–45 ml/2–3 tablespoons butter. Fry some oysters in a single layer until lightly browned on one side, then turn over and cook until other side is lightly browned. Remove from the frying pan and keep warm while you fry the remaining oysters. Add a little more butter to the frying pan and fry next batch. Continue until all the oysters are fried. Serve the oysters with lemon wedges and Cocktail Sauce (page 121).

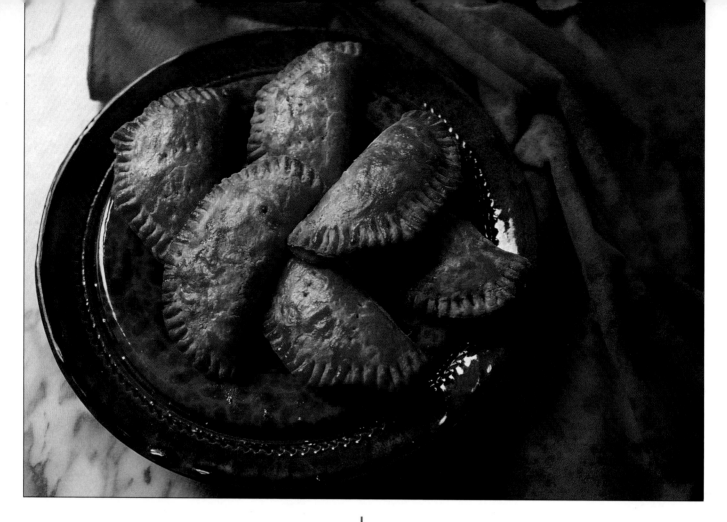

TWO-BITE MEAT PIES

You can fill these savoury miniature turnovers with almost anything – Dirty Rice (page 78), Crawfish Pie filling (page 55), or the fillings listed below. Once filled these can be baked or deep-fried, but I recommend the lower-fat baked version. Serve these hot for snacking during card games or football-watching parties.

MAKES ABOUT 24 PIES

PASTRY

275 g/10 oz plain flour
pinch of salt
50 g/2 oz cold butter
50 g/2 oz lard
2 eggs, lightly beaten
45–60 ml/3–4 tbsp cold milk

GLAZE

1 egg, lightly beaten
60 ml/2 fl oz milk

OVEN TEMPERATURE: 190°C/375°F/Gas Mark 5

≈ Sift together the flour and salt. Using a pastry cutter or a pair of sharp knives, cut in the shortenings until the flour is the consistency of cornmeal. Add the eggs and mix well. Add the milk, 15 ml/1 tablespoon at a time, until the dough sticks together and forms a ball.

≈ Wrap the dough in cling film and refrigerate for at least 1 hour. Meanwhile, make the filling of your choice.

≈ Return dough to room temperature before rolling out.

≈ Roll out the dough 3 mm/⅛ inch thick. With cutter or inverted glass, cut the dough into circles 75–100 cm/3–4 inches in diameter. Gather up the scraps, roll out again and cut out circles, repeating until all the dough is all used.

≈ Put 15 ml/1 tablespoon filling in the centre of each circle. Fold each circle in half, pinch the edges together to seal.

≈ Place each on lightly greased baking sheet. Mix the egg and milk together, and brush across tops of the pies. Bake at 190°C/375°F/Gas Mark 5 until the pastry is lightly browned, about 20 minutes. Serve hot.

IF YOU USE A FOOD PROCESSOR:

≈ Mix all the ingredients together, except the milk. Then place the dough in a bowl, add 15 ml/1 tablespoon of milk at a time and mix gently with your hands until dough sticks together and forms a ball. If you add the milk in the food processor, you won't be able to feel when the dough is moist enough, and will probably add too much milk.

SPICY PORK AND BEEF FILLING

For a spicier filling, substitute a jalapeño chilli for the mild one specified in the recipe.

ENOUGH FILLING FOR ABOUT 24 PIES

30 ml/2 tbsp vegetable oil
1 onion, chopped
3 cloves garlic, finely chopped
1 mild chilli, chopped
225 g/8 oz minced pork
225 g/8 oz minced beef
1 tomato, seeded and chopped
100 g/4 oz grated raw potato
5 ml/1 tsp salt
5 ml/1 tsp ground cumin
7.5 ml/1½ tsp fresh thyme or 2.5 ml/½ tsp dried
7.5 ml/1½ tsp fresh oregano or 2.5 ml/½ tsp dried
30 ml/2 tbsp chopped fresh coriander
175 ml/6 fl oz beef stock (page 16)

≈ In large frying pan, heat the oil. Sauté the onion, garlic and chilli until onion is golden, about 10 minutes. Add the meat and cook until browned. Add the tomato, potato, seasonings and stock and mix well. Lower the heat and simmer 10 minutes. Taste and adjust the seasonings. Set aside and let cool before using.

PORK AND TASSO FILLING

This is a chunky filling in a spicy, savoury sauce.

ENOUGH FILLING FOR ABOUT 24 PIES

30 ml/2 tbsp vegetable oil
450 g/1 lb pork, diced into 5 mm/¼-inch pieces
100 g/4 oz Tasso, diced
100 g/4 oz lard
50 g/2 oz plain flour
225 g/8 oz chopped onion
1 stalk celery, chopped
½ green pepper
600 ml/1 pt beef stock
1.5 ml/¼ tsp dried sage
1.5 ml/¼ tsp cayenne
1.5 ml/¼ tsp black pepper
10 ml/2 tsp fresh thyme or 2.5 ml/½ tsp dried
10 ml/2 tsp dry mustard

≈ In a medium frying pan, heat the oil. Sauté the pork and Tasso until browned. Set aside.
≈ In medium saucepan, make a peanut-butter-coloured roux of the lard and flour (page 15). Remove from the heat and stir in the vegetables. Return to the heat and cook until the vegetables are wilted, about 5 minutes.
≈ In a small saucepan, bring the beef stock to the boil and add the seasonings. Gradually add the stock to the roux, whisking after each addition. Stir in the pork and Tasso. Simmer until mixture is slightly thickened, about 15 minutes. Set aside and let cool before using.

CRAB-STUFFED MUSHROOMS

These mushrooms are very rich and very delicious. Even people who usually think they do not like seafood will love this stuffing.

MAKES 24

24 large fresh mushrooms
25 g/1 oz butter
4 spring onions, chopped
1 clove garlic, finely chopped
2.5 ml/½ tsp salt
1.5 ml/¼ tsp cayenne
25 g/1 oz dry breadcrumbs
60 ml/2 fl oz double cream
350 g/12 oz fresh crab meat, picked over, or frozen or tinned, well drained
Parmesan cheese

OVEN TEMPERATURE: 180°C/350°F/Gas Mark 4

≈ Clean the mushrooms and separate the stems from the caps. Meanwhile, finely chop the stems. Steam the mushrooms for 5 minutes, then set aside.

≈ In a frying pan over medium heat, melt the butter. Add the chopped stems, spring onions and garlic and cook until most of the liquid is evaporated, 8–10 minutes. Add the salt, cayenne, breadcrumbs and cream, and mix well. Gently stir in the crab meat and cook until just heated through.

≈ Stuff the mushroom caps with the crab mixture, mounding a little on each top. Sprinkle each with Parmesan cheese. Arrange on a lightly greased baking sheet. Bake at 180°C/350°F/Gas Mark 4 for 10 minutes, then broil 2–3 minutes until the cheese turns golden brown.

FROGS' LEGS

These frogs' legs are dipped in two breading mixtures, then quickly deep-fried in very hot oil so they don't become greasy. I like to serve them as appetizers, with tartar sauce on the side, but I serve more than one appetizer so my more squeamish friends – the ones who aren't reassured that frogs' legs taste like chicken – have something to eat.

SERVES 6–12 AS APPETIZERS

900 g/2 lbs frogs' legs
225 g/8 oz plain flour
5 ml/1 tsp salt
2.5 ml/½ tsp black pepper
2.5 ml/½ tsp cayenne
5 ml/1 tsp onion powder
5 ml/1 tsp garlic powder
2 eggs, lightly beaten
175 ml/6 fl oz milk
250 g/9 oz cornmeal
75 g/3 oz cornflour
5 ml/1 tsp salt
1.5 ml/¼ tsp black pepper
1.5 ml/¼ tsp cayenne
vegetable oil for frying

≈ Wash the frogs' legs and pat dry on kitchen paper. Set aside.

≈ Set out 3 bowls. In the first bowl, combine the flour, salt, pepper, cayenne and onion and garlic powders. In the second bowl, mix the eggs and milk, together. In the third bowl, combine the cornmeal and remaining ingredients, except the oil.

≈ Dip the frogs' legs first in flour mixture, then shake off the excess. Next, dip the frogs' legs in the egg mixture, then in the cornmeal mixture, again shaking off the excess.

≈ In a deep frying pan or wok, heat 5–7.5 cm/2–3 inches of oil to 180°C/360°F. Fry the legs in small batches so they are not crowded. Cook for 7 minutes, turning once. Remove from the oil, drain briefly, then place on kitchen paper and keep warm in the oven while you fry the remaining legs. Make sure the oil returns to 185°C/360°F before frying the next batch.

RIGHT Located in northeastern Louisiana near St. Joseph, Lake Bruin was developed as a State Park in the 1950s around a beautiful oxbow lake, once part of the Mississippi River. The park is famed for the old cypress trees growing from the lake itself and for its excellent fishing and boating waters.

CAJUN POPCORN

Little prawn or crawfish tails are dipped in a spicy flour batter, then deep-fried to make these tasty tidbits. Serve with Tartar Sauce (page 121), Mustard Sauce (pages 122–123) or Cocktail Sauce (page 121) for dipping. And, be sure to make plenty.

SERVES 6–8

25 g/1 oz cornflour
25 g/1 oz plain flour
30 ml/2 tbsp cornmeal
5 ml/1 tsp salt
2.5 ml/½ tsp onion powder
2.5 g/½ tsp garlic powder
1.5 g/¼ tsp cayenne
large pinch black pepper
2 eggs, lightly beaten
15 g/½ oz butter, melted
60 ml/6 fl oz warm beer
900 g/2 lbs small prawns, shelled and deveined, or crayfish tails, shelled
vegetable oil for frying

≈ Combine all the dry ingredients. Whisk in the eggs, butter and beer together until smooth. Refrigerate at least 3 hours to give the gluten in the flour a chance to expand. Whisk again before using.

≈ In a deep frying pan or wok heat 4 cm/1½ inches of oil to 180°C/350°F. Pat the prawns dry, then dip in the batter. Drop some of the prawns in the oil, but don't crowd, and fry until golden brown, turning once, about 2 minutes total. Drain well on kitchen paper and keep warm while frying the remaining prawns. Be sure the oil returns to 180°C/350°F before frying the next batch. Continue until all the prawns are fried.

SHRIMP SALSA

SHRIMP SALSA

A cool, easy dip for savoury biscuits, crisps or vegetables. Make a couple hours in advance to let the flavours blend. Taste again just before serving and adjust the Tabasco sauce. For a hot salsa, use a jalapeño chilli.

2 medium tomatoes, seeded and chopped
½ cucumber, peeled, seeded and diced
3 spring onions, finely chopped
1 mild chilli, seeded and finely chopped
30 ml/2 tbsp chopped fresh coriander
22.5 ml/1½ tbsp olive oil
22.5 ml/1½ tbsp cider vinegar
dash of salt
few drops of Tabasco sauce
100 g/4 oz tiny brown shrimps, cooked and cleaned

≈ In a bowl, combine all the ingredients and refrigerate for at least 2 hours before serving.

HOT CRAB SPREAD

This creamy dip, served hot, is delicious with savoury biscuits or raw vegetables. I recommend fresh crab meat but frozen or tinned are acceptable.

3 tbsp soured cream
75 g/3 oz cream cheese
15 ml/1 tbsp fresh-squeezed lemon juice
2.5 ml/½ tsp prepared horseradish
15 ml/1 tbsp chopped fresh dill
2 spring onions, finely chopped
dash of salt
dash of fresh-ground black pepper
175 g/6 oz fresh crab meat, picked over

OVEN TEMPERATURE: 180°C/350°F/Gas Mark 4

≈ Cream the soured cream and cream cheese together with an electric beater. Add the remaining ingredients, except the crab, and beat until smooth. Gently stir in the crab.
≈ Put the mixture in an ovenproof serving dish and bake at 180°C/350°F/Gas Mark 4 until hot, about 15 minutes.

CAJUN DEVILLED EGGS

HOT CRAB SPREAD

CAJUN DEVILLED EGGS

The Tasso gives these devilled eggs their spicy taste. If you don't have Tasso, use another ham, but add cayenne and paprika to give it a Cajun flavour.

MAKES 6

6 eggs, hard-boiled and shelled
25 g/1 oz Tasso, finely chopped
15 ml/1 tbsp finely chopped green pepper
1 spring onion, finely chopped
2.5 ml/½ tsp fresh-squeezed lemon juice
30 ml/2 tbsp mayonnaise
30 ml/2 tbsp Dijon-style mustard
dash of fresh-ground pepper
1–2 drops of Tabasco sauce

≈ Cut the eggs in half lengthways. Remove the yolks and put them in a small bowl and set aside the whites. Mash the yolks with a fork. Add the remaining ingredients to the yolks and mix well with a fork. Taste and adjust the seasonings. Spoon the mixture into the egg whites.

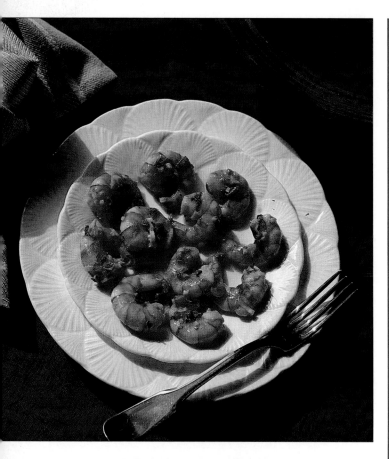

COLD PRAWNS IN HORSERADISH SAUCE

These pungent, spicy prawns are easy to make and have the advantage of being prepared in advance. Serve as an appetizer, with lots of toothpicks and napkins on the side.

SERVES 4–6

30 ml/2 tbsp cider vinegar
30 ml/2 tbsp lemon juice
45 ml/3 tbsp olive oil
2 cloves garlic, finely chopped
45 ml/3 tbsp chopped spring onions
30 ml/2 tbsp finely chopped fresh parsley
5 ml/1 tsp red-pepper flakes
5 ml/1 tsp Creole mustard
30 ml/2 tbsp Dijon-style mustard
30 ml/2 tbsp prepared horseradish
2.5 g/½ tsp celery seed
450 g/1 lb medium cooked prawns, shelled and deveined

≈ In a bowl, combine all the ingredients, except the prawns, and mix well. Add the prawns making sure each piece is well coated. Refrigerate for at least 3 hours or as long as 24 hours.

CAJUN BBQ PRAWNS

It is a tradition of Cajun cooking that BBQ prawns never see a grill. Instead, they are briefly cooked in a buttery sauce so spicy that the shells are left on during cooking, as protection for the diner, and then peeled by hand as they are eaten. I like to serve these as an appetizer, with lots of bread on the side for dipping in the leftover sauce. Although this recipe is spicy hot, it is not as palate-searing as some Cajun recipes.

SERVES 6–8

350 g/12 oz unsalted butter
6 garlic cloves, finely chopped
15 ml/1 tbsp chopped fresh basil or 15 ml/1 tsp dried
10 ml/2 tsp fresh rosemary or 2.5 ml/½ tsp dried
7.5 ml/1½ tsp fresh oregano or 2.5 ml/½ tsp dried
250 ml/8 fl oz seafood stock (page 17)
20 ml/4 tsp fresh-squeezed lemon juice
15 ml/1 tbsp Worcestershire sauce
2.5 ml/½ tsp salt
10 ml/2 tsp cayenne
5 ml/1 tsp paprika
10 ml/2 tsp dry mustard
5 ml/1 tsp red-pepper flakes
675 g/1½ lbs medium unshelled prawns

≈ In a heavy saucepan over low heat, melt the butter, swirling occasionally and taking care that butter does not brown. As soon as the butter starts to melt, add the garlic and herbs, and continue swirling until butter is completely melted.

≈ Add the remaining ingredients, except the prawns, and use a wire whisk to mix well. Simmer over low heat to allow flavours to blend, about 15 minutes. Add the prawns and cook just until prawns are opaque and curled, 5–7 minutes. Remove from heat and pour carefully into a heat-proof serving dish.

SALADS

TOMATO-BASIL SALAD

Take advantage of the ripe tomatoes and surplus of basil from summer gardens with this cool and elegant – but simple – salad. Drizzle with Vinagrette (page 123), a combination of balsamic vinegar and a high-quality olive oil, or your favourite dressing.

SERVES 4

4 large, ripe tomatoes, sliced
bunch of fresh basil
4–6 thin slices of red onion (available at specialist greengrocers and some large supermarkets)
salt to taste
fresh-ground black papper

≈ Slice the tomatoes, salt lightly, and let them drain on kitchen paper for about 20 minutes.

≈ Wash the basil and dry well with kitchen paper or in a salad spinner. Tear the leaves from the stems and arrange a thin layer of leaves on a platter. Top with about half the tomato slices. Separate the onion rings and scatter about half over the tomatoes. Add another layer of basil, tomatoes and onions. Sprinkle lightly with fresh-ground black pepper, and garnish with a few extra basil leaves.

VARIATION:

≈ Top the tomatoes with thin slices of fresh mozzarella cheese.

PRAWN SALAD

This chilled salad uses prawns, artichoke hearts and olives, and is topped with a creamy and tangy, but reduced-calorie, dressing.

SERVES 4

Lettuce, spinach, or a combination of both
450 g/1 lb prawns, cooked, shelled, deveined and chilled
2 large or 3 medium whole artichoke hearts, cooked, chilled and sliced
75 g/3 oz pitted ripe olives
2 ripe tomatoes, cut into wedges
75 g/3 oz sliced mushrooms

DRESSING

175 ml/6 fl oz low-fat plain yoghurt
45 ml/3 tbsp mayonnaise, preferably reduced-calorie
45 ml/3 tbsp buttermilk
7.5 ml/1½ tsp fresh-squeezed lemon juice
1 spring onion, finely chopped
30 ml/2 tbsp Dijon-style mustard
salt to taste
fresh-ground white pepper to taste

≈ To make the dressing, whisk all the ingredients together and refrigerate until ready to serve. The dressing tastes better if you allow several hours for flavours to blend.

≈ Arrange a bed of greens on each of 4 salad plates. Divide the prawns, artichoke slices, olives, tomatoes, and mushrooms among the 4 plates and top with the dressing and fresh-ground black pepper, if desired.

BELOW The Blessing of the Fleet at the annual festival held in Morgan City to honour the economic lifeblood of the area – the shrimp (prawn) and petroleum industries.

CORN SALAD

Marinated and served cold, this salad is a great way to use up any leftover vegetable in your refrigerator. Use fresh corn if its available, or substitute frozen corn.

SERVES 6

450 g/1 lb corn kernels (7–8 fresh ears)
50 g/2 oz carrot, thinly sliced
50 g/2 oz courgette, thinly sliced
12 cherry tomatoes, halved
1 green pepper, chopped
½ small red onion, thinly sliced
75 g/3-oz tin ripe olives, drained
15 ml/1 tbsp capers

DRESSING

90 ml/6 tbsp olive oil
45 ml/3 tbsp white wine vinegar
5 ml/1 tsp fresh lemon juice
5 ml/1 tsp Dijon-style mustard
15 ml/1 tbsp fresh tarragon
2.5 ml/½ tsp salt
1.5 ml/¼ tsp black pepper
large pinch cayenne

≈ Cook corn in boiling water until tender, about 3 minutes, then drain. Rinse with cold water and drain again. Mix with all the salad ingredients in a bowl.

≈ In a bottle or small bowl, mix together all the dressing ingredients. Shake or whisk to mix thoroughly. Pour over salad and stir to coat. Refrigerate several hours.

COLESLAW

This tangy cabbage salad provides a cool counterpart to Fried Catfish (page 59), Cajun BBQ Prawns (pages 30–31) or Blackened Redfish (pages 56–57). Use a combination of red and white cabbage for colour. Prepare this several hours in advance to give flavours time to blend.

SERVES 4

275 g/10 oz shredded cabbage
3 carrots, peeled and grated
3 spring onions, finely chopped
½ large green pepper, cut into thin strips
120 ml/4 fl oz mayonnaise
120 ml/4 fl oz soured cream
60 ml/2 fl oz white wine vinegar
15 ml/1 tbsp sugar
15 ml/1 tbsp chopped fresh parsley
5 ml/1 tsp celery seed
15 ml/1 tbsp grated onion
pinch of salt
pinch of fresh-ground black pepper

≈ In a salad bowl, combine the vegetables and toss together well.

≈ In a small bowl, whisk together the remaining ingredients, then taste and adjust seasonings. Mix with the slaw, cover and refrigerate until ready to serve.

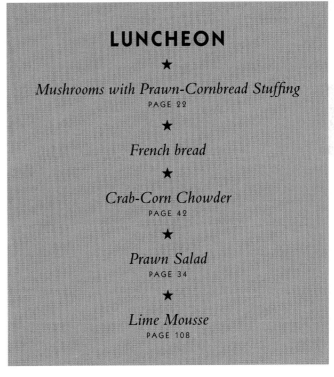

LUNCHEON

★

Mushrooms with Prawn-Cornbread Stuffing
PAGE 22

★

French bread

★

Crab-Corn Chowder
PAGE 42

★

Prawn Salad
PAGE 34

★

Lime Mousse
PAGE 108

SPICY CHICKEN SALAD WITH MUSHROOMS

SPICY CHICKEN SALAD WITH MUSHROOMS

The subtle taste of mushrooms, the tang of oranges and the nutty taste of pecans complement the spicy chicken in this salad.

SERVES 4

5 ml/1 tsp salt
2.5 ml/½ tsp cayenne
2.5 ml/½ tsp black pepper
1.5 ml/¼ tsp fresh thyme
1 uncooked chicken breast, skinned and cut into strips
30 ml/2 tbsp vegetable oil
275 g/10 oz torn lettuce or salad greens
75 g/3 oz sliced mushrooms
50 g/2 oz pecans
2 Satsuma oranges, sectioned, or one 300 g/11-oz tin mandarin orange sections

≈ In a small bowl, mix the spices together. Toss the chicken in the spices, until chicken is well coated.
≈ In a frying pan, heat the oil, sauté the chicken until brown all over. Drain well on kitchen paper and refrigerate the chicken until ready to serve.
≈ In a salad bowl, toss the greens, mushrooms, pecans, oranges and chicken. Serve with a favourite dressing.

POTATO SALAD

Soured cream and fresh dill flavour this salad made with unpeeled potatoes. You can serve it chilled, but I like it best when the potatoes are still slightly warm so the flavours are not masked.

SERVES 6–8

900 g/2 lbs small red potatoes, unpeeled
mayonnaise
soured cream
2.5 ml/½ tsp salt
1.5 ml/¼ tsp black pepper
2.5 ml/½ tsp dry mustard
30 ml/2 tbsp chopped fresh parsley
30 ml/2 tbsp chopped fresh dill
1 stalk celery, diced
4 spring onions, chopped
3 hard-boiled eggs, diced

≈ Drop the potatoes into boiling water and cook until fork tender, 20–30 minutes, depending on their size. Drain well and let sit until cool enough to handle.
≈ While the potatoes are cooking, make a dressing by whisking together the mayonnaise, soured cream, salt, pepper, mustard, parsley and dill.
≈ Cube the potatoes and mix with the celery, onions and eggs. Gently stir in the dressing. Taste and adjust seasonings.

POTATO SALAD

COLD JAMBALAYA SALAD

This salad is a great make-ahead dish, and a great way to use up leftovers. For an elegant dish, mound the salad on a serving platter or a pretty ceramic tart tin, then circle it with wedges of tomatoes and/or lemons, and top it with several large cooked prawns and a sprig of parsley.

SERVES 6

15 g/½ oz butter
chopped onions
1 clove garlic, finely chopped
40 g/1½ oz diced cooked ham
5 ml/1 tsp salt
1.5 ml/¼ tsp cayenne
1 bay leaf
225 g/8 oz white rice
30 ml/2 tbsp good-quality olive oil
15 ml/1 tbsp wine or balsamic vinegar
15 ml/1 tbsp fresh-squeezed lemon juice
few drops of Tabasco sauce, if desired
3 spring onions, chopped
2 stalks celery, chopped
1 small green pepper, chopped
2 medium tomatoes, seeded and cut into bite-size chunks
675 g/1½ lbs any combination of cooked prawns, crab or chicken

≈ In a medium saucepan, melt the butter. Sauté the onions and garlic until wilted, about 5 minutes. Add 475 ml/16 fl oz water, the ham and seasonings, and bring to the boil. Stir in the rice and return to the boil. Reduce the heat to very low, cover and cook until liquid is absorbed and the top of the rice is pitted with steam holes, 15–20 minutes. Fluff the rice with a fork. Cover, remove from the heat and let sit for 5–10 minutes. Chill or let sit until cold. Remove the bay leaf.

≈ In a large bowl, toss the rice with the olive oil, vinegar, and lemon juice. Taste and adjust flavourings, and add Tabasco sauce if desired. Stir in the remaining ingredients, garnish and serve.

SOUPS AND STEWS

—★—

OYSTER STEW

Essentially oysters cooked in cream, this rich 'stew' is deceptively easy.

SERVES 4

25 g/1 oz butter
4 spring onions, finely chopped
1 stalk celery, finely chopped
1.1 l/2 pts single cream
2.5 ml/½ tsp salt
1.5 ml/¼ tsp cayenne
10 ml/2 tsp Worcestershire sauce
3 dozen large or 4 dozen small-medium oysters with their juice, large oysters halved
butter or sherry for garnishing

≈ In a medium saucepan over low heat, melt the butter. Sauté the spring onions and celery until limp, about 5 minutes.

≈ Add the single cream, salt, cayenne and Worcestershire sauce and heat until the soup just starts to boil. Lower the heat, add the oysters and their liquor, and cook just until the edges of the oysters start to curl, 2–3 minutes. Taste and adjust the seasonings.

≈ You may garnish each bowl with a pat of butter or a dash of sherry, if you like.

PRAWN AND LEEK BISQUE

This rich, creamy bisque starts with a flavourful prawn stock, so buy prawns with the heads on if you can find them. It's important to make your own stock for this soup, so it picks up the delicate flavour of leeks. If you can't find prawns with heads, get some extra shells to make the stock with. I like to make the soup, up through the point of puréeing, early in the day, then reheat and add the cream just before serving.

SERVES 6

350g/12 oz medium prawns, shelled and deveined with heads and shells reserved
1 large carrot, unpeeled, cubed
2 stalks celery, leaves and all, sliced
2 leeks, including green tops, sliced
2–3 sprigs of fresh parsley
2 bay leaves
5 black peppercorns
40 g/3 tbsp butter
1 leek, white part only, chopped
2 cloves garlic, finely chopped
450 g/1 lb sliced mushrooms
30 ml/2 tbsp minced fresh parsley
1 bay leaf
5 ml/1 tsp salt
10 ml/2 tsp chopped fresh basil
5 ml/1 tsp chopped fresh thyme
large pinch white pepper
large pinch black pepper
large pinch cayenne
2.5 ml/½ tsp dry mustard
45 ml/3 tbsp plain flour
350 ml/12 fl oz double cream
30 ml/2 tbsp sherry

≈ Put the prawn heads and shells, carrot, celery, leeks, parsley, bay leaves and peppercorns in a large pot. Add 900 ml/1½ pts water. Make a mental note of the water level in the pot, because you will need at least 900 ml/1½ pts of stock after it has simmered for several hours. Add another 900 ml–1.75 l/1½–3 pts water, enough to cover the prawn shells and vegetables by several inches. Bring to the boil. Skim off the grey foam. Reduce heat and simmer, un-covered, for 2–3 hours, adding extra water if necessary to keep at least 900 ml/1½ pts liquid in the pot.

≈ Strain the stock, discarding the prawn heads, shells and vegetables. Measure 900 ml/1½ pts stock into a small saucepan; freeze or refrigerate any remaining stock for future use. Return 900 ml/1½ pts of stock to the stove and keep warm over a low heat.

≈ In a frying pan, melt the butter. Sauté the leek, garlic and mushrooms about 10 minutes. Add the vegetables to the stock with the seasonings. Bring to the boil, then reduce the heat and simmer, uncovered, 15 minutes. Add the prawns and simmer just until prawns are opaque and tightly curled.

≈ Purée the soup in a blender or food processor; you will probably have to do this in several batches. (At this point you may refrigerate the puréed soup for several hours. Reheat before continuing.)

≈ Whisk the flour into the cream, then add to the soup. Heat just short of the boiling point. Taste and adjust seasonings. Add the sherry.

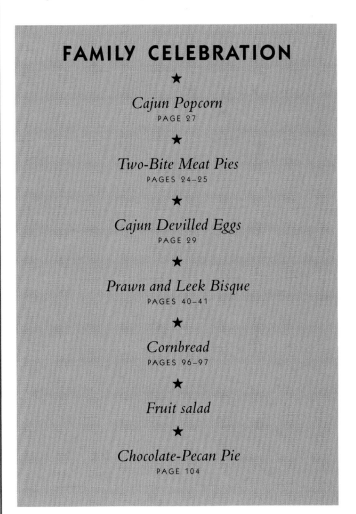

FAMILY CELEBRATION

★

Cajun Popcorn
PAGE 27

★

Two-Bite Meat Pies
PAGES 24–25

★

Cajun Devilled Eggs
PAGE 29

★

Prawn and Leek Bisque
PAGES 40–41

★

Cornbread
PAGES 96–97

★

Fruit salad

★

Chocolate-Pecan Pie
PAGE 104

YELLOW SQUASH AND POTATO SOUP

A smooth, thick broth is poured over bits of browned potato in this rich, yet inexpensive, soup. If you want to make ahead, refrigerate after puréeing, then reheat and add the cream just before serving.

SERVES 4

25 g/1 oz butter
100 g/4 oz onion, chopped
1 clove garlic, finely chopped
2 baking potatoes, cubed but not peeled
2–3 yellow courgettes, sliced
750 ml/1¼ pts poultry stock (page 16) or tinned broth
pinch of cayenne
pinch of fresh-ground black pepper
5 ml/1 tsp paprika
2.5 ml/½ tsp thyme
2.5 ml/½ tsp basil
salt to taste
175 ml/6 fl oz single cream

≈ In a frying pan over medium heat, melt the butter. Sauté the onion and garlic until wilted, about 5 minutes. Add the potatoes and saute 8–10 minutes. (You may need to add another 15 ml/1 tbsp of butter at this point.) Remove 100 g/4 oz potatoes and keep warm. Add the squash to the frying pan and sauté about 3 minutes.

≈ In a saucepan, mix together the poultry stock and seasonings, then add the sautéed vegetables. Bring to the boil, then reduce the heat and simmer about 40 minutes. Purée the soup in batches in a blender or food processor.

≈ Return the puréed soup to the saucepan and heat through. Add the cream and salt to taste and heat through but do not boil. Divide the reserved potatoes among serving bowls and ladle the soup over the potatoes.

BELOW A long avenue of ancient oaks leads to Oak Alley Plantation, Vacherie, a landmark of antebellum | *architecture with its Doric columns and two-story colonnaded veranda.*

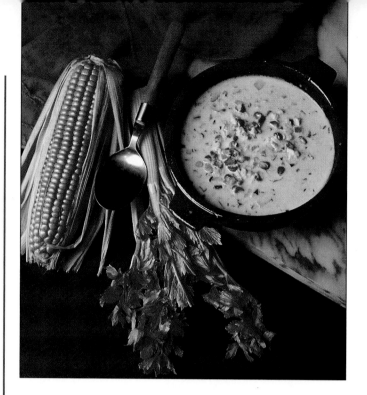

CRAB-CORN CHOWDER

My favourite recipe in this book. The soup has a wonderful rich taste.

SERVES 4

25 g/2 tbsp butter
½ onion, chopped
1 stalk celery, finely chopped
1 clove garlic, finely chopped
350 ml/2 fl oz seafood stock (page 17)
120 ml/4 fl oz dry white wine or poultry stock (page 16)
175 g/6 oz fresh or frozen corn kernels
1.5 ml/¼ tsp dried thyme
2.5 ml/½ tsp salt
dash of cayenne
1.5 ml/¼ tsp white pepper
250 ml/8 fl oz single cream
120 ml/4 fl oz soured cream
100 g/4 oz crab meat
15 ml/1 tbsp chopped fresh parsley
2 spring onions, chopped

≈ In a large saucepan over low heat, melt the butter. Sauté the onion, celery and garlic until wilted, about 5 minutes.

≈ Add the seafood stock and wine and bring to the boil. Add the corn and spices. Return to the boil, then reduce the heat and simmer, uncovered, about 20 minutes. Stir in the cream and continue simmering for 10 minutes but do not boil. Whisk in the soured cream. Add the crab meat, parsley and spring onions, and heat just enough to warm the crab. Do not allow to boil.

CREAM OF ARTICHOKE SOUP

Start with fresh artichoke because this delicious soup uses the water in which the artichokes are cooked for extra flavour. Canned artichokes do not give the same rich flavour.

SERVES 4–6

STOCK

2 large or 3 medium globe artichokes
15 ml/1 tbsp lemon juice
2.5 ml/½ tsp salt
30 ml/2 tbsp olive oil
2 garlic cloves, crushed

SOUP

25 g/1 oz butter
100 g/4 oz onion, finely chopped
250 ml/8 fl oz reserved artichoke cooking water
475 ml/16 fl oz chicken stock or tinned broth
reserved artichoke scrapings
large pinch cayenne
30 ml/2 tbsp fresh basil
20 g/¾ oz plain flour
350 ml/12 fl oz double cream
reserved sliced artichoke hearts
salt to taste

≈ Cut most of the stem off the artichokes, leaving only a 1 cm/½-inch stub. Bend the outer petals back until they snap off, leaving the meat at the bottoms of the leaves attached to the heart. Continue snapping off leaves until you've removed several rows, then with a large knife, slice off the remaining artichoke just above the base of the remaining leaves. Collect the discarded leaves and stems in a large bowl or bag.

≈ In a medium saucepan over high heat, bring 950 ml/2 pts water to the boil. Add the lemon juice, salt, olive oil, garlic and artichoke hearts and simmer until the hearts can be easily pierced with a fork, but are still firm, not mushy, 20–25 minutes.

≈ Remove the hearts from the water and save 250 ml/8 fl oz of the cooking water, discarding the rest. When the artichoke hearts are cool enough to handle, use a spoon to scoop the chokes out of the centres. With a sharp knife, trim away the stringy remains of any leaves around the edges. Slice the hearts and set aside.

≈ Place the reserved leaves and stems in a large pot, cover with water and bring to the boil, then lower the heat and simmer 20–25 minutes. Drain and allow the leaves to cool. When they are cool enough to handle, scrape the flesh from the bottoms of the leaves and reserve. Remove the stringy exteriors of the stems and slice the soft insides into a bowl with the leaf scrapings.

≈ In a small frying pan over medium heat, melt the butter. Sauté the onions until wilted, about 5 minutes. Set aside.

≈ In a medium saucepan, bring the aritchoke cooking water and chicken stock to the boil. Lower the heat and add the artichoke scrapings, cayenne and basil, then simmer 5 minutes.

≈ Mix the flour with a little of the cream and stir until smooth. Whisk the soup until smooth, then whisk in the remaining cream. Bring to just below the boiling point, then add the artichoke slices. Taste and adjust the salt.

CRAWFISH BISQUE

Crawfish Bisque is a very special time-consuming dish, but the results are delicious. The bodies of the crawfish are stuffed with a cornbread stuffing, then cooked in the bisque to absorb the broth. Served over rice, this bisque is a filling main dish. The best part comes at the bottom of the bowl, when the soup is gone and the stuffed crawfish remain. Holding the shell in one hand, scoop out the stuffing with your spoon. Yum!

At a minimum, cook the crawfish, make the stock and bake the cornbread a day in advance – and then plan to spend most of the next day in the kitchen, too.

SERVES 4–6

STOCK

1 large onion, sliced
1 lemon, sliced
2 garlic cloves, crushed
3 fresh parsley sprigs
1 stalk celery, including leaves, sliced
2 whole cloves
15 ml/1 tbsp whole mustard seed
5 ml/1 tsp celery seed
2 bay leaves
2.5 ml/½ tsp red-pepper flakes
5 ml/1 tsp black pepper
5 ml/1 tsp salt
2.25 kg/5 lbs whole crawfish

≈ Add all the ingredients, except the crawfish, to a large stockpot of boiling water and boil for 15–20 minutes to develop the flavour, then add the crawfish. Return to the boil, then simmer for 20 minutes. Remove the crawfish with tongs and plunge into cold water. Return the stock to a low heat to simmer while you clean the crawfish.

≈ To clean the crawfish, twist off the tails from the bodies, and cut out all the tail meat. Save the tail meat in 1 bowl. Remove the yellow fat from the bodies and save the fat in a second bowl. Pull the body shells – the thorax – free from the innards, and break off eyes and beaks. Save the best shells for stuffing. Place the innards, any small or broken shells, the heads and the remains of the tail shells in the stock, and continue simmering for total cooking time of 2 hours.

≈ Strain the stock, discarding the vegetables and shells. Reserve 1.25 l/2¼ pts stock: freeze any leftover stock for future use.

STUFFED CRAWFISH

4–5 crawfish bodies per person
25 g/1 oz butter
100 g/4 oz onion, chopped
50 g/2 oz spring onions, chopped
½ green pepper, chopped
1 stalk celery, chopped
2 cloves garlic, finely chopped
15 ml/1 tbsp chopped fresh parsley
5 ml/1 tsp fresh thyme or 1.5 ml/¼ tsp dried
2.5 ml/½ tsp salt
large pinch black pepper
few drops of Tabasco sauce
5 ml/1 tsp lemon juice
1 egg, lightly beaten
100 g/4 oz finely crumbled cornbread (pages 96–97)
½ reserved crawfish tail meat, ground or finely chopped
½ reserved crawfish fat
reserved crawfish stock (see above) to moisten, if necessary

OVEN TEMPERATURE: 180°C/350°F/Gas Mark 4

≈ Thoroughly clean the crawfish shells, removing any bits of innards that remain. Let dry on kitchen paper.

≈ In a large frying pan, melt the butter over low heat. Sauté the onions, green pepper, celery and garlic, 5 minutes. Remove from the heat, and put in a bowl with the remaining ingredients, except the stock. The stuffing should be moist enough that it sticks together when you roll some into a small ball: it should not be mushy. Add some more stock if needed.

≈ Fill the crawfish shells with cornbread mixture, pressing the stuffing so it is solid and not crumbly. Put the stuffed shells on an ungreased baking sheet and bake at 180°C/ 350°F/Gas Mark 4 for 10 minutes. Remove from oven and set aside.

RIGHT This stately mansion, built in 1830 on the banks of the Bayou Teche, New Iberia, was once the center of a great plantation. Framed by magnolias and ancient live oaks dripping with Spanish moss, Shadows-on-the-Teche is now owned by the National Trust for Historic Preservation.

BISQUE

60 ml/4 tbsp plain flour
50 g/2 oz lard
1 medium tomato, seeded and chopped
1 stalk celery, chopped
1 clove garlic, finely chopped
100 g/4 oz onion, chopped
½ green pepper, chopped
1.25 l/2¼ pts reserved crawfish stock (see above)
½ reserved crawfish tail meat
½ reserved crawfish fat
5 ml/1 tsp fresh thyme or 1.5 ml/¼ tsp dried
1 bay leaf
5 ml/1 tsp Worcestershire sauce
2.5 ml/½ tsp salt
1.5 ml/¼ tsp black pepper
large pinch cayenne
5 ml/1 tsp fresh-squeezed lemon juice
reserved stuffed crawfish shells (see above)
350 g/12 oz cooked rice to serve
100 g/4 oz spring onions, chopped

≈ Make a dark, mahogany-coloured roux of lard and flour (page 15). Remove from heat and stir in the tomato, celery, garlic, onion and green pepper. Return to very low heat and cook until vegetables are limp, about 5 minutes. Set aside.

≈ In a large pot, bring the crawfish stock to the boil. Add the roux and vegetables to the stock 1 spoonful at a time, whisking to mix thoroughly. Add the crawfish tail meat, fat, seasonings and lemon juice. Gently, with tongs or large spoon, add the stuffed shells to soup. Simmer 45 minutes, uncovered.

≈ Put rice in bottom of each bowl. Fish out the stuffed shells and divide among the bowls. Add the spring onions to the soup, then ladle the bisque into the bowls.

CRAWFISH BISQUE

GUMBOS AND JAMBALAYAS

———★———

CHICKEN AND ANDOUILLE SAUSAGE GUMBO

The spicy flavour of this roux-based gumbo comes from the Andouille sausage and the seasonings in the chicken. Taste before serving and adjust seasonings.

SERVES 6

25 g/1 oz plain flour
5 ml/1 tsp salt
2.5 ml/½ tsp black pepper
1.5 ml/¼ tsp cayenne
5 ml/1 tsp paprika
2.5 ml/½ tsp onion powder
2.5 ml/½ tsp garlic powder
3 whole or 6 half uncooked chicken breasts, skinned and cubed
60 ml/2 fl oz vegetable oil
100 g/4 oz plain flour
225 g/8 oz lard
450 g/1 lb chopped onion
2 medium green peppers, chopped
3 stalks celery, chopped
1.75 l/3¼ pt poultry stock (page 16)
350 g/12 oz Andouille sausage, cubed
2 garlic cloves, finely chopped
350 g/12 oz cooked rice to serve

≈ Mix 45 ml/3 tbsp flour with the seasonings in a small bowl, then toss the chicken until the cubes are well coated with spices. Heat the oil in a large frying pan and sauté the chicken until browned. Drain on kitchen paper, if necessary. Set aside.

≈ Combine the remaining flour and the lard to make a dark, mahogany-coloured roux (page 15). Remove the roux from the heat and add the chopped vegetables. Stir until the roux stops darkening. Return to the heat and cook until the vegetables are limp, about 5 minutes.

≈ Add the poultry stock, a little at a time, stirring until well blended. Bring to the boil, then add the chicken, Andouille and garlic. Reduce the heat and simmer for 1 hour. You may wish to skim the gumbo occasionally if fat from the roux or the sausage rises to the top. Taste and adjust seasonings. Serve over rice.

GUMBO

MUCH OF THE HISTORY OF CAJUNS AND THEIR COOKING IS MIXED *into the stew they call gumbo. Like many kinds of Louisiana food, gumbo traces its lineage to a French dish, bouillabaise, a fish stew. The name gumbo is derived from the word 'kingombo', a type of okra, the seeds of which Africans brought with them on slave ships. Filé, powdered sassafras leaves that are used as a seasoning and a thickener, was contributed by the Choctaw Indians. Spanish settlers added red peppers. And instead of Mediterranean fish, lobster and eels, Gulf of Mexico fishermen used prawns, crab and oysters.*

≈ Almost any kind of meat, fish or game can be used in gumbo: roast beef, alligator, frogs' legs, hot links or other sausages, eggs and dried prawns are some of the more unusual ingredients. More common are fresh prawns, crab, oysters, crawfish, redfish, chicken, duck and spicy Andouille sausage.

≈ Most gumbos begin with roux, a slow-cooked mixture of lard and flour that adds flavour, colour and body to the stew. Then come chopped vegetables – and a rich stock, simmered most of the day from prawn shells, crab carcasses or chicken parts. Gumbo is spicy, although not as hot as its cousin, jambalaya.

≈ Okra can also be used to thicken gumbo, and health-conscious people use it instead of roux. Filé powder is another thickener that is added only after the gumbo has finished cooking and is removed from the heat, or is sprinkled into serving bowls. Cooking the filé powder gives it an unpleasant flavour, and it will turn gumbo dark and stringy.

≈ Traditionally, gumbo is ladled over cooked white rice in wide, shallow bowls.

SEAFOOD GUMBO WITH OKRA

Okra is used as the thickener, so this gumbo is lighter than a roux-based gumbo. It is only mildly spicy. Use at least three different type of fish and shellfish, in whatever combination of fresh seafood is available: prawns, crab, oysters, frogs' legs, crawfish tails, clams, mussels, scallops, or filleted redfish, red snapper, cod or other fish, cut into cubes.

SERVES 8

30 ml/2 tbsp vegetable oil
450 g/1 lb onions, chopped
2 large green peppers, chopped
2 stalks celery, chopped
3 garlic cloves, finely chopped
3 large or 4 medium tomatoes, seeded and chopped
250 g/8-oz tin tomato sauce
1.75 l/3 pts seafood stock (page 17)
15 ml/1 tbsp fresh-squeezed lemon juice
2 bay leaves
15 ml/1 tbsp fresh thyme or 5 ml/1 tsp dried
5 ml/1 tsp salt
1.5 ml/¼ tsp black pepper
large pinch cayenne
large pinch white pepper
2.5 ml/½ tsp paprika
675 g/1½ lbs okra, thawed and well drained if frozen, sliced
900 ml/2 lbs mixed seafood (see introduction)
450 g/1 lb cooked rice to serve
filé powder, optional

≈ In a large frying pan, heat the oil. Sauté the onion, pepper, celery and garlic until limp, about 5 minutes. Transfer to a large saucepan or stockpot and add the tomatoes, tomato sauce, seafood stock, lemon juice and seasonings. Bring to the boil, then reduce the heat and simmer, uncovered, 5 minutes.

≈ Add the okra and return to the boil, then reduce the heat and simmer 30 minutes. Add the seafood: cubed fish and frogs' legs take the longest times to cook, oysters the least.

≈ Spoon the rice into individual large bowls. Ladle the gumbo over the rice. If desired, add a pinch of filé powder to each bowl.

CHICKEN, ANDOUILLE AND SHRIMP JAMBALAYA

CASUAL DINNER PARTY

★

Cajun BBQ Prawns with lots of French bread
PAGES 30–31

★

Green salad

★

Chicken and Andouille Sausage Gumbo
PAGE 47

★

Sweet-Potato and Pecan Pie
PAGE 105

ABOVE *The Afton Villa Gardens lie just north of St. Francisville, which is located 35 miles north of Baton Rouge on the Mississippi River. The gardens were once part of a* plantation on which stood a beautiful French Gothic-style villa, built in the mid-1800s. The villa survived the Civil War only to burn down in the 1960s.

DUCK, OYSTER AND ARTICHOKE GUMBO

The delicate flavours of duck, oysters and artichokes are combined in this roux-based gumbo. It is a two-day job to roast the duck and make stock, then to make the gumbo, but the product of all that time and effort is a rich and hearty stew.

SERVES 8

1 domestic duck
100 g/4 oz lard
50 g/2 oz plain flour
225 g/8 oz onion, chopped
225 g/8 oz green pepper, chopped
2 stalks celery, chopped
2 cloves garlic
1.75 l/3 pts duck stock (see below)
375 g/12 oz reserved cooked duck meat
15 ml/1 tbsp fresh basil or 1 tsp. dried
2.5 ml/½ tsp dry mustard
5 ml/1 tsp salt
2.5 ml/½ tsp black pepper
1.5 ml/¼ tsp cayenne
5 ml/1 tsp paprika
7.5 ml/1½ tsp fresh thyme or 2.5 ml/½ tsp dried
4 artichoke hearts, cooked and sliced (see Cream of Artichoke Soup, page 43)
1 dozen oysters, shelled and cut into bite-size pieces
4 spring onions, chopped
50 g/2 oz chopped fresh parsley
450 g/1 lb cooked rice to serve

≈ Roast the duck as directed on pages 70–71, omitting the onion, spice and orange juice mixture. Cut the meat from the bones, chop and refrigerate the meat: you will need about 375 g/12 oz meat for this recipe. Make a stock from the carcass as directed on page 16.

≈ In a medium saucepan, make a dark, mahogany-coloured roux of lard and flour (page 15). Remove from the heat and add the onion, pepper, celery and garlic. Stir until the roux stops darkening. Return to the heat and cook until the vegetables are limp, about 5 minutes.

≈ In large saucepan or stockpot, bring the duck stock to the boil. Add the roux, 1 large spoonful at a time, whisking after each addition until well blended. Add the duck meat and seasonings, then simmer 40 minutes. Add the artichokes and simmer 5 minutes more. Add the oysters, spring onions and parsley, and cook until the edges of the oysters start to curl, 2–3 minutes. Spoon the rice into large individual bowls. Ladle the gumbo over the rice.

CHICKEN, ANDOUILLE AND PRAWN JAMBALAYA

All the spiciness in this jambalaya comes from the meat. Be sure to taste before you serve, and adjust seasonings, especially if you've had to substitute other ham or sausage for the Tasso and Andouille. This level is what I call baseline spiciness. It's hot to most people, but not as spicy as traditional Cajun cooking, so add more black and cayenne pepper if you like mouth-searing food.

SERVES 6–8

5 ml/1 tsp salt
2.5 ml/½ tsp cayenne
2.5 ml/½ tsp black pepper
7.5 ml/1½ tsp fresh or 2.5 ml/½ tsp dried thyme
1 whole or 2 half uncooked chicken breasts, skinned and cubed
30 ml/2 tbsp vegetable oil
3 stalks celery, chopped
2 medium onions, chopped
2 medium green peppers, chopped
2 garlic cloves, finely chopped
100 g/4 oz Tasso or other smoked ham, chopped
150 g/6 oz Andouille or other spicy sausage, sliced
450 g/1 lb tomatoes, seeded and chopped
225 g/8-oz tin tomato sauce
250 ml/8 fl oz poultry or seafood stock (pages 16–17)
225 g/8 oz medium shrimp, shelled and deveined
100 g/4 oz spring onions, chopped
575 g/1¼ lb cooked rice to serve

≈ In a small bowl, mix together the salt, cayenne, black pepper and thyme. Toss the chicken, until it is well coated with spices.

≈ In a large frying pan or Dutch oven, heat the oil. Sauté the chicken, stirring almost constantly, until the chicken is browned, 6–8 minutes. Add the celery, onion, green pepper and garlic, and sauté until the vegetables are limp, about 5 minutes.

≈ Add the Tasso, Andouille sausage, tomatoes, tomato sauce and stock and stir and cook until mixture is bubbling. Reduce the heat and simmer until tomatoes have cooked down and liquid is slightly reduced, creating a rich, red broth. Add the prawns and cook until the prawns are opaque and tightly curled, 2–3 minutes. Taste and adjust the seasonings. It should be very spicy. Add the spring onions and enough rice so that the mixture is neither soupy nor dry.

NOTE:

≈ If you did not cook the rice with salt, you will need to increase the amount of salt in the jambalaya.

SEAFOOD JAMBALAYA

Jambalaya is traditionally made with ham, but it's not a necessity. I make this jambalaya for a friend who doesn't eat meat. You may add ham back in, if you desire – 100–225 g/4–8 oz chopped ham – and if you use Tasso ham, you may need to decrease the seasonings.

SERVES 6–8

30 ml/2 tbsp vegetable oil
1 onion, chopped
1 green pepper, chopped
2 stalks celery, chopped
3 cloves garlic, finely chopped
3 large tomatoes, seeded and chopped
250 ml/8 fl oz tin tomato sauce
250 ml/8 fl oz seafood stock (page 17)
50 g/2 oz chopped fresh parsley
2 bay leaves
15 ml/1 tbsp fresh thyme or 5 ml/1 tsp dried
5 ml/1 tsp salt
1.5 ml/¼ tsp black pepper
2.5 ml/½ tsp cayenne
large pinch white pepper
900 g/2 lbs fresh prawns, crab meat, crawfish or oysters, or any combination, prepared
100 g/4 oz spring onions, chopped
450 g/1 lb cooked rice to serve

≈ In a deep frying pan or Dutch oven, heat the oil. Sauté the onion, green pepper, celery and garlic until vegetables are limp, about 5 minutes. Add the tomatoes, tomato sauce, stock, parsley and seasonings and simmer gently until the tomatoes are cooked down and some of the liquids have reduced. Taste and adjust the seasonings.

≈ Add the seafood. (If using oysters, cut into bite-sized pieces and add in last 2–3 minutes of cooking.) Simmer just until the prawns are opaque and tightly curled, 5–7 minutes. Just before serving, mix in the spring onions. Serve over rice.

NOTE:

≈ If the rice is not cooked with salt, you will need additional salt in the jambalaya.

JAMBALAYA

THERE ARE ALL SORTS OF THEORIES ABOUT THE ORIGIN OF THE word jambalaya, but the most common one is that it comes from the Spanish word jamon, *meaning ham, or the French word* jambon, *also meaning ham. So it's not surprising that virtually all jambalaya recipes include at least a little ham, even if it is (horrors!) turkey ham.*

≈ *Jambalaya is a descendant of Spanish paella, which was brought to Louisiana during the Spanish occupation of the late 18th century. But instead of the saffron that colours paella a golden yellow, Cajuns use cayenne to season jambalaya.*

≈ *Jambalaya is a sort of hash. There are some requisite ingredients – rice, spices, a little ham, lots of tomatoes, onions, celery and green peppers – but other additions can be any meat or seafood leftovers in your refrigerator. Most common are shellfish, chicken, and sausage, but just about anything else is acceptable, from spareribs to rabbit to alligator.*

≈ *Most jambalaya is made on the stovetop, but once the vegetables are sautéed and the liquids are hot, it can be mounded into a large casserole dish and baked. Many recipes call for uncooked rice to be added while the jambalaya is still sloshing with liquids, but I prefer to add cooked rice until I get just the texture and consistency I want. Otherwise, if there's just a little less liquid than you think, the rice can absorb it all and still be slightly crunchy, while you're left with a dry jambalaya.*

RIGHT While New Orleans is the urban centre of Louisiana, the capitol sits to the north at Baton Rouge on the Mississippi River, surrounded by 27 acres of formal gardens.

SEAFOOD

—★—

CRAWFISH PIE

Paprika colours the rich-and-creamy filling pink in this recipe. If you can find crawfish tails already peeled and cooked, buy them. You're in for a lot of work if you have to cook and clean enough whole crawfish to produce enough tail meat for this recipe. Use your favourite piecrust recipe, or the one for Two-Bite Meat Pies (page 24).

SERVES 6–8

50 g/2 oz lard
25 g/1 oz plain flour
100 g/4 oz onion, chopped
1 large stalk celery, chopped
½ large green pepper, chopped
2 garlic cloves, finely chopped
30 ml/2 tbsp chopped fresh parsley
120 ml/4 fl oz seafood stock (page 17) or clam juice
350 ml/2 fl oz single cream
5 ml/1 tsp paprika
4 ml/¾ tsp fresh thyme or ¼ tsp dried
7.5 ml/1½ tsp chopped fresh basil or ½ tsp dried
1.5 ml/¼ tsp black pepper
1.5 ml/¼ tsp cayenne
large pinch white pepper
5 ml/1 tsp salt
10 ml/2 tsp fresh-squeezed lemon juice
675 g/1½ lbs crawfish tails, shelled and cooked
6 spring onions, chopped
pastry dough for 2-crust pie

OVEN TEMPERATURE: 190°C/375°F/Gas Mark 5

≈ In a heavy saucepan, make a peanut-butter-coloured roux of lard and flour (page 15). Remove from the heat, add the vegetables, garlic and parsley. Return to the heat, and cook until the vegetables are wilted, about 5 minutes.

≈ In another pan, heat the seafood stock and single cream to a slow boil. Whisk in the roux, 1 large spoonful at a time, whisking after each addition. Add the seasonings and lemon juice and bring to the boil, then reduce the heat and simmer for 20 minutes. Add the crawfish tails and spring onions. Taste and adjust the seasonings, then let cool to lukewarm.

≈ Roll out the piecrust dough and line a 23 cm/9-inch pie tin with half the dough, sprinkling a little flour over the bottom to prevent sogginess. Add filling and top with the second crust. Trim and seal the edges, pinching into a fluted edge.

≈ Bake at 190°C/375°F/Gas Mark 5 until the crust is golden brown, about 30 minutes. Let cool about 10 minutes before serving.

BLACKENED REDFISH

The sudden and huge popularity of blackened redfish in the mid-1980s created a shortage of redfish, especially outside the American South. Fortunately, this recipe can be used with many other types of fish, as long as they have strong connective tissue and are no thicker than 2 cm/¾ inch. Red snapper, tilefish, sea bass, pompano, salmon and catfish fillets all work well. Most recently, I used a New Zealand sea bass that was delicious.

≈ This method uses an extremely hot frying pan and will set off your smoke alarm. Open a window, turn on the ventilation system and keep a tight-fitting lid close at hand to smother any flame-ups – they are common. For that reason, don't try this if you have an above-stove microwave oven. You must use a cast-iron frying pan: the high temperature will ruin any other. A charcoal barbecue will not get the pan hot enough.

≈ In spite of all these warnings and instructions, blackened fish is an easy and quick dish, and the results are delicious. I recommend getting one small, extra fillet the first time you try this, and experimenting with it, just to get a feel for the method.

≈ This dish requires all your attention. You may want to have an extra pair of hands in the kitchen to make side dishes and the butter sauce just before serving. Otherwise, make your side dishes and butter sauce before you begin cooking, then reheat the sauce (preferably in a microwave) to melt the butter at serving time.

≈ Use onion and garlic powder and dried herbs instead of fresh in this recipe because the high cooking temperature gives fresh herbs and garlic an unpleasant burned taste. The fish can be from 100–350 g/4–12 oz each, depending on appetites, but no more than 2 cm/¾ in thick, and the more uniform the thickness, the better.

SERVES 6

6 fish fillets
175 g/6 oz unsalted butter, melted

SEASONING MIX:

7.5 ml/1½ tsp salt
15 ml/1 tbsp paprika
5 ml/1 tsp onion powder
5 ml/1 tsp garlic powder
5 ml/1 tsp dried thyme
2.5 ml/½ tsp dried oregano
2.5 ml/½ tsp black pepper
5 ml/1 tsp cayenne

BUTTER SAUCE:

100 g/4 oz unsalted butter, melted
15 ml/1 tbsp fresh-squeezed lemon juice
1 spring onion, finely chopped
2.5 ml/¼ tsp cayenne
2.5 ml/¼ tsp salt

≈ Put a cast-iron frying pan over high heat and heat until the pan begins to smoke and white ash forms on the bottom, at least 10 minutes. If after 20 minutes, there is no ash, your stove may not produce enough heat. Sprinkle a few drops of water in the pan. If they dance, the frying pan is hot enough to do the job, but cooking may take an extra 30 seconds a side.

≈ Combine all the ingredients for the seasoning mix and set aside.

≈ Combine all the ingedients for butter sauce and set aside.

≈ Dip the fillets in plain melted unsalted butter, then sprinkle the seasoning mix on both sides and pat into the butter. The butter will congeal on the cold fish and may flake off. If it does, put it in pan with the barest side up and spoon some melted butter over the bare spots. But be wary: the butter is likely to flame up during cooking. If it does, put a lid on the frying pan to smother the fire, then continue.

≈ When the pan is ready, put 2 fillets in, moving quickly and cook until the bottoms are blackened, up to 2 minutes. (The fish will not be solid black, but ridges, edges and grains of seasonings will be blackened.) Turn over. If the thickness is not uniform, you may wish to press down gently with a spatula during cooking. Again, cook until ridges on bottom are blackened, up to 2 minutes. The interior of the fish should be opaque but juicy. Keep warm in a low oven while you repeat with the remaining fillets.

≈ Reheat the butter sauce if necessary and pour over the fish. Serve at once.

PECAN CATFISH

PECAN CATFISH

Instead of flour or cornmeal, these easy catfish fillets are baked in a ground-pecan coating. The flavour is deliciously set off by soured cream, mustard and spring onions.

SERVES 4

60 ml/2 fl oz Dijon-style mustard
60 ml/2 fl oz soured cream
30 ml/2 tbsp milk
4 spring onions, finely chopped
100 g/4 oz finely ground pecans
4 catfish fillets, skinned, about 175 g/6 oz each

OVEN TEMPERATURE: 240°C/475°F/Gas Mark 9

≈ In a large, shallow bowl, mix together the mustard, soured cream, milk and spring onions. Dip the catfish fillets in the mustard mixture: the mixture is a little thick, so you may need to spread some on any bare spots. Carefully dredge the fillets in the ground pecans.

≈ Place the fillets on a greased baking sheet and bake until opaque but still juicy, 8–10 minutes.

SUMMER DINNER PARTY

★

Hot Crab Spread with savoury biscuits and crudites
PAGES 28–29

★

Cold Prawns in Horseradish Sauce
PAGE 30

★

Corn Salad
PAGE 34

★

Spicy Green Beans
PAGE 91

★

Cornbread
PAGES 96–97

★

Pecan Catfish
PAGES 58–59

★

Peach-Amaretto Ice Cream
PAGE 109

FRIED CATFISH

Catfish are cheap and plentiful in the United States, especially since they are now raised on commercial catfish farms. These fillets are quartered, so the thickest parts are on the edges and cook more evenly. The fillets are deep-fried, but if you prefer, you can pan-fry them, as long as you cook them a little longer. Serve with lemon wedges and Tartar Sauce (page 121), accompanied by Hushpuppies (page 95) and Coleslaw (page 35) or Corn Salad (page 34).

SERVES 4

50 g/2 oz plain flour
2.5 ml/½ tsp salt
2.5 ml/½ tsp black pepper
large pinch cayenne
2.5 ml/½ tsp paprika
5 ml/1 tsp dry mustard
1 egg, lightly beaten
175 ml/6 fl oz milk
few drops of Tabasco sauce
100 g/4 oz cornmeal
25 g/1 oz cornflour
25 g/1 oz plain flour
2.5 ml/½ tsp salt
2.5 ml/½ tsp black pepper
2.5 ml/½ tsp cayenne
2.5 ml/½ tsp onion powder
2.5 ml/½ tsp garlic powder
4 catfish fillets, about 175 g/6 oz each, skinned and quartered
vegetable oil for frying

≈ Set out 3 bowls. In the first bowl, combine the plain flour, salt, pepper, cayenne, paprika and dry mustard. In the second bowl, mix the egg and milk together and add a few drops of Tabasco sauce. In the third bowl, combine the cornmeal and remaining ingredients, except the catfish and oil.

≈ Dip the catfish pieces first in the flour mixture, then shake off the excess. Next, dip the catfish in the egg mixture, then in the cornmeal mixture, again shaking off the excess. (You may also put the 2 breading mixtures in paper or plastic bags, and shake the catfish in the bags to coat.)

≈ In deep frying pan or wok, heat 3 inches of oil to 180°C/350°F. Add a few pieces of breaded catfish, making sure you don't crowd them and cook until golden brown, turning once, 1½–2 minutes a side. Drain well on kitchen paper and keep warm in the oven while you fry the remaining catfish. Make sure the oil returns to 180°C/350°F before frying the next batch.

ALMOND TROUT

The classic method for preparing this dish is to coat the trout with flour or breadcrumbs, then pan-fry them. I prefer to grill my trout with just a little olive oil and paprika, then add the crunchy topping of almonds and spring onions. The result is a simpler dish with a wonderful flavour that saves a few calories.

SERVES 2

2 small trout, about 450 g/1 lb each, filleted with the heads removed (can be whole or in 2 pieces)
30 ml/2 tbsp olive oil
2.5 ml/½ tsp paprika
40 g/1½ oz butter
75 g/3 oz sliced blanched almonds
5 ml/1 tsp Worcestershire sauce
10 ml/2 tsp fresh-squeezed lemon juice
5 ml/1 tsp grated lemon peel
few drops of Tabasco sauce
3 spring onions, chopped
30 ml/2 tbsp chopped fresh parsley

Spray a grill pan with a non-stick spray. Put the trout on the rack, skin side down. Combine the olive oil and paprika, and brush over filleted meat. Put under the hot grill, about 5 inches from the heat, and grill unskinned side up until opaque but still juicy, 5–6 minutes, using a rule of 10 minutes per 2.5 cm/1 in of the fillet's thickness.

≈ While fish is cooking, in a small frying pan, melt the butter. Add the almonds and cook until they are a golden brown. Add the Worcestershire sauce, lemon juice, lemon peel and Tabasco sauce and mix well. Remove from the heat, add the spring onions and parsley, and quickly spoon over the grilled trout.

BARBECUED SHARK

This barbecue recipe is an easy and tasty way to cook shark, or other dense-fleshed fish such as swordfish. I think it is delicious plain, but you can also serve it with dilled Butter Sauce for Fish (page 124.)

SERVES 4

45 ml/3 tbsp fresh-squeezed lemon juice
45 ml/3 tbsp fresh-squeezed lime juice
2.5 ml/½ tsp grated lemon peel
2.5 ml/½ tsp grated lime peel
60 ml/2 fl oz olive oil
45 ml/3 tbsp chopped fresh dill
3 garlic cloves, finely chopped
pinch of salt
4 shark steaks, about 175 g/6 oz each
fresh-ground black pepper

≈ In a glass or other non-reactive dish, combine all the ingredients, except the shark and pepper. Place the shark steaks in the marinade, turning to coat thoroughly, and spreading dill and garlic bits over tops of the fish. Sprinkle with fresh-ground black pepper, cover with cling film and refrigerate about 2 hours, turning once or twice.

≈ When the barbecue coals have stopped flaming, place the shark steaks on a lightly greased grill. Cook about 5 minutes each side, turning once. (Total cooking time should be about 10 minutes per inch of thickness.) Baste with the extra marinade, if desired. The fish is cooked through when the flesh turns opaque, but is still juicy.

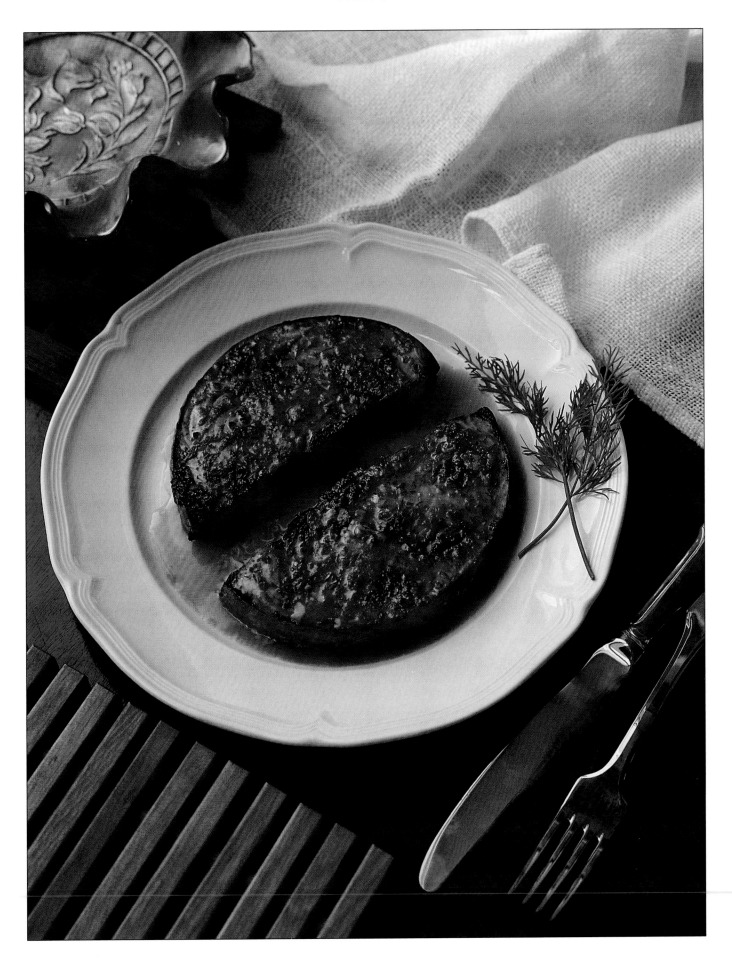

CRAB-STUFFED FISH

Use whole trout, red snapper, red mullet, plaice or sole for this dish, cooked individually if you use small fish. Or, present an elegant platter of a large, stuffed fish surrounded by lemon slices and parsley sprigs. Fresh crab meat is best but frozen or canned are acceptable. If you wish, serve with Butter Sauce for Fish (page 124.)

SERVES 4

25 g/1 oz butter
6 spring onions, chopped
100 g/4 oz coarsely chopped mushrooms
15 ml/1 tbsp chopped fresh parsley
1 clove garlic, finely chopped
1.5 ml/¼ tsp salt
1.5 ml/¼ tsp paprika
1.5 ml/¼ tsp black pepper
30 ml/2 tbsp grated Parmesan chees
60 ml/2 fl oz double or single cream
225 g/8 oz fresh crab meat, picked over
4 whole fish, about 225 g/8 oz each, cleaned and boned
salt to taste
fresh-ground black pepper to taste
flour for dredging (optional)
olive oil or melted butter

OVEN TEMPERATURE: 180°C/350°F/Gas Mark 4

≈ In a small frying pan, melt the butter. Sauté the onions, mushrooms, parsley and garlic until limp, about 5 minutes. Stir in the salt, paprika, pepper, Parmesan, and cream until well mixed. Add the crab, stirring gently. Set aside.

≈ Rinse the fish and pat dry with kitchen paper. Season the insides lightly with salt and pepper. You may dredge the trout in flour at this point, covering the outside only with a thin coat of flour, and shaking off excess. The flouring step is optional.

≈ Stuff with the crab mixture, then skewer the fish closed with toothpicks, or sew a few large stitches with coarse thread. Put the fish in a lightly oiled baking tin and brush with olive oil or drizzle with melted butter.

≈ Bake the fish at 180°C/350°F/Gas Mark 4 until the flesh at thickest point is opaque but is still juicy, about 10 minutes. Do not wait for the fish to flake easily, because it continues cooking after it is removed from the oven, and would be overcooked by the time you serve it.

NOTE:

≈ If you use one large fish, a 1.25–1.5 kg/2½–3 lb. fish will serve 4–5 people.

CRAWFISH ÉTOUFFÉE

Etouffée means 'smothered' in French, and here a rich, spicy roux-based sauce smothers the crawfish. The sauce can be made ahead of time, then reheated and the crawfish added just before serving.

SERVES 4–6

100 g/4 oz lard
50 g/2 oz plain flour
225 g/8 oz onion, chopped
1 large green pepper, chopped
1 large stalk celery, chopped
4 cloves garlic, finely chopped
4 medium tomatoes, seeded and chopped
75 g/3 oz fresh parsley, chopped
475 ml/16 fl oz seafood stock (page 17)
2.5 ml/½ tsp cayenne
2.5 ml/½ tsp black pepper
5 ml/1 tsp salt
7.5 ml/1½ tsp black pepper
5 ml/1 tsp salt
7.5 ml/1½ tsp fresh thyme or 2.5 ml/½ tsp dried
675 g/1½ lbs crawfish tails, shelled and cooked
8 spring onions, chopped
225–350 g/8–12 oz cooked rice to serve

≈ In a heavy saucepan, make a mahogany-coloured roux of the lard and flour (page 15.) Remove from the heat, stir in the vegetables and parsley. Return to the heat and cook until the vegetables are limp, about 5 minutes.

≈ In large saucepan, bring the seafood stock to a slow boil. Add the roux and vegetables, 1 spoonful at a time, whisking after each addition until the mixture is smooth. Add the seasoning. Reduce the heat and simmer for 30 minutes.

≈ Add the crawfish tails and simmer until crawfish is heated through, about 5 minutes. Just before serving, stir in the spring onions. Serve over rice.

CRAWFISH ÉTOUFFÉE

PRAWN CREOLE

Whenever possible, start with whole prawns and use the prawn heads and shells to make a rich seafood stock for this dish. You can make the sauce ahead of time, then reheat and add the prawns just before serving. This recipe is only mildly spicy, so add more cayenne or Tabasco sauce if you want a fiery dish.

SERVES 6

30 ml/2 tbsp vegetable oil
225 g/8 oz onion, chopped
1 large green pepper, chopped
2 stalks celery, chopped
3 garlic cloves, finely chopped
450 g/1 lb fresh tomatoes, seeded and chopped
250 ml/8 fl oz can tomato sauce
120 ml/4 fl oz dry red wine or seafood stock (page 17)
350 ml/12 fl oz seafood stock (page 17)
50 ml/1 tsp salt
2 bay leaves
30 ml/2 tbsp chopped fresh parsley
15 ml/1 tbsp chopped fresh basil or 5 ml/1 tsp dried
7.5 ml/1½ tsp fresh thyme or 2.5 ml/½ tsp dried
2.5 ml/½ tsp black pepper
1.5 ml/¼ tsp cayenne
few drops of Tabasco sauce
15 ml/1 tbsp fresh-squeezed lemon juice
450 g/1 lb medium prawns, shelled and deveined
6 spring onions, chopped
350 g/12 oz cooked rice to serve

≈ In a large saucepan, heat the oil. Sauté 100 g/4 oz onions until golden. Add the remaining onions, green pepper, celery and garlic, and sauté until vegetables are limp, about 5 minutes.

≈ Add the tomatoes, tomato sauce, wine, stock, seasonings, Tabasco sauce and lemon juice. Bring to the boil, stir well, then reduce the heat and simmer 30 minutes.

≈ Just before serving, add the prawns and spring onions, and cook just until prawns are opaque and tightly curled, 5–7 minutes. Serve over rice.

LIME-GRILLED PRAWNS

Light on fat and heavy on flavour, this is an easy and delicious barbecue recipe.

SERVES 6

120 ml/4 fl oz peanut oil
60 ml/2 fl oz fresh-squeezed lime juice
4 cloves garlic, finely chopped
30 ml/2 tbsp chopped fresh coriander
2.5 ml/½ tsp red-pepper flakes
2.5 ml/½ tsp salt
1.5 ml/¼ tsp black pepper
675 g/1½ lbs medium prawns, shelled and deveined

≈ In a glass or another non-reactive bowl, mix together all the ingredients, except the prawns, until well combined. Add the prawns, turning to make sure each is thoroughly coated, then refrigerate for several hours, turning once or twice. If you're using wooden skewers, soak the skewers in water for at least 1 hour while prawns are marinating. This helps prevent the skewers burning.

≈ Thread the prawns on the skewers; they should not touch each other. When the coals have stopped flaming, place the skewers on the grill, directly over the coals. Cook just until prawns are opaque and tightly curled, 2–3 minutes a side, turning once. Don't overcook or the prawns will toughen.

BOILED PRAWNS

Here is a basic recipe for cooking prawns that are to be eaten cold with a dip, rémoulade sauce or in a salad. Whether you shell them before you cook them is a matter of personal preference. If you like, you can also use wine or beer as the cooking liquid, and you can increase the amount of chilli flakes if you like your prawns spicy.

MAKES 1 LB.

2 carrots, sliced
1 onion, sliced
2 cloves garlic, crushed
1 bay leaf
parsley sprigs
5 ml/1 tsp salt
15 ml/1 tbsp whole mustard seed
5 ml/1 tsp black pepper
1.5 ml/¼ tsp dried chilli flakes
1 lemon, sliced
450 g/1 lb prawns

≈ In a large saucepan, bring 2.5 l/4½ pts water to the boil. Add the carrots, onion, garlic, bay leaf and parsley and continue boiling about 10 minutes to release the vegetables' flavours into the cooking liquid. Add the spices and lemon and boil for another 2 minutes.

≈ Add the prawns and boil just until the prawns are opaque and tightly curled, 2–3 minutes. Do not overcook or the prawns will become tough. Drain and refrigerate, or put on ice.

THE FLAVOUR OF NEW ORLEANS

LEFT *The Old Absinthe House, located among the burlesque clubs of Bourbon Street, is named for the licorice-flavoured green spirit it served before absinthe was banned in the United States.*

ABOVE *This streetcar named Desire, a namesake of the Tennessee Williams play set in New Orleans, sits in the French Quarter.*

RIGHT *New Orleans is famous for the elaborate iron grillework of its balconies.*

TOP *Like Louisiana's food, its music is a blend of competing cultural strains. New Orleans jazz emerged from Dixieland, rhythm and blues, African drums, Caribbean calypso, and gospel choirs. Its landmarks include the clubs of Bourbon Street and Preservation Hall, the city's best-known jazz club.*

RIGHT *The Pontalba Apartments in New Orleans' French Quarter were built in 1850 and are believed to be the oldest apartment buildings in America. The four-story, red-brick buildings are still such a prestigious address that there is a lengthy waiting list for vacancies.*

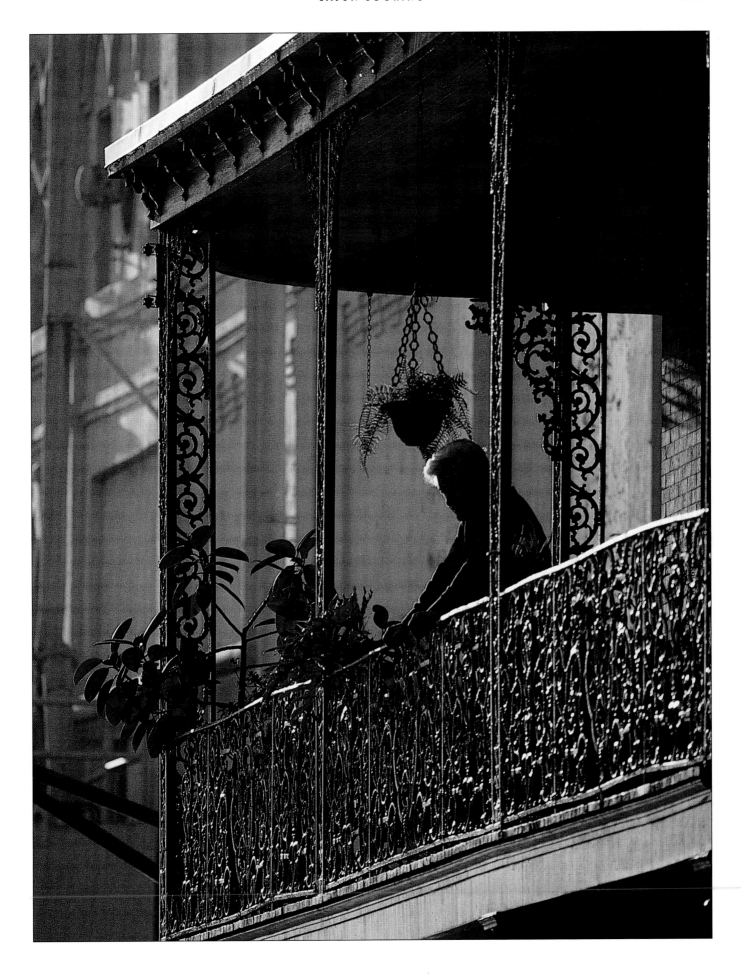

MEAT AND POULTRY

———★———

MUSTARD-BAKED CHICKEN

Coated with a sauce of mustard and soured cream, this chicken dish is easy and tasty.

SERVES 6-8

120 ml/4 fl oz soured cream
60 ml/2 fl oz Creole mustard
175 g/6 oz finely crumbled cornbread (pages 96–97)
7.5 ml/1½ tsp fresh thyme or ½ tsp dried
5 ml/1 tsp salt
1.5 ml/¼ tsp black pepper
1.5 ml/¼ tsp cayenne
2 chickens, about 1.25–1.5 kg/2½–3 lbs each, cut into serving pieces
60 ml/2½ oz butter, melted

OVEN TEMPERATURE: 190°C/375°F/Gas Mark 5

≈ In a small bowl, combine the soured cream and mustard. In another small bowl, mix together the cornbread crumbs and seasonings.

≈ Spread the mustard mixture over the chicken pieces, then roll the chicken in the crumb mixture. Arrange the chicken in a single layer in large, shallow baking dish and drizzle with the melted butter. Bake at 190°C/375°F/Gas Mark 5 until the chicken is golden brown and the juices run clear if tested with the tip of a knife, about 1 hour.

BAKED VEAL CHOPS WITH RICE AND PRAWNS STUFFING

This flavourful dish has a lot of steps, but is not difficult to make.

STUFFING

15 g/½ oz butter
50 g/2 oz chopped onion
1 clove garlic, finely chopped
475 ml/16 fl oz beef stock (page 16) or tinned broth
2.5 ml/½ tsp grated lemon peel
2.5 ml/½ tsp salt
1.5 ml/¼ tsp black pepper
7.5 ml/1½ tsp fresh thyme or 2.5 ml/½ tsp dried
175 g/6 oz brown rice
50 g/2 oz wild rice
25 g/1 oz butter
½ small green pepper, chopped
1 stalk celery, chopped
4–5 spring onions, chopped
175 g/6 oz prawns, cooked, shelled, deveined and coarsely chopped

≈ In a small frying pan over medium heat, melt 15 ml/½ oz butter. Sauté the onion and garlic about 5 minutes.

≈ In medium saucepan, bring the beef stock to the boil. Add the onion and garlic, lemon peel, seasoning and rices. Return to the boil, then reduce the heat very low, cover and cook until all liquid is absorbed, about 50 minutes.

≈ In frying pan on medium heat, melt 25 g/1 oz butter. Sauté the green pepper and celery until limp, about 5 minutes. Add the spring onions and sauté 1 minute longer. Add the vegetables and prawns to the rice, and set aside.

VEAL CHOPS

4 thick veal chops, each at least 2–2.5 cm/¾–1 in. thick
50 g/2 oz plain flour
2.5 ml/½ tsp salt
large pinch pepper
1.5 ml/¼ tsp paprika
1.5 ml/¼ tsp onion powder
1.5 ml/¼ tsp garlic powder
45–60 ml/3–4 tbsp vegetable oil
120–250 ml/4–8 fl oz beef stock (page 16) or tinned broth

OVEN TEMPERATURE 180°C/350°F/Gas Mark 4

≈ Cut a gash on the side of each veal chop, to make a pocket.

≈ Mix together the flour and seasonings in a bowl or paper sack. Dip the chops in the flour.

≈ In a large frying pan over high heat, heat the oil. Add the chops and cook until lightly browned on each side, then remove from heat.

≈ Spoon some rice stuffing into the pocket of each veal chop. Place the chops in a shallow baking tin and pour in enough beef stock by 5 mm/¼ in. Cover the pan and bake at 180°C/350°F/Gas Mark 4 until meat is tender and all traces of pink are gone, about 1 hour. Serve extra stuffing on the side.

ROAST DUCK

Because domestic ducks are so fatty, I roast them unstuffed so the fat that cooks out doesn't overpower the taste of the stuffing. Serve this duck with Baked Crawfish–Cornbread Stuffing (page 97) on the side, or use the meat in Duck With Prawns and Fettucine (page 81), a duck salad or Duck Rice (page 77).

SERVES 4

1 domestic duck, about 1.75–2.25 kg/4–5 lb.
5 ml/1 tsp salt
2.5 ml/½ tsp black pepper
5 ml/1 tsp dry mustard
5 ml/1 tsp garlic powder
2.5 ml/½ tsp dried sage
1 onion, quartered
30 ml/2 tbsp vegetable oil
1 onion, chopped
2 cloves garlic, finely chopped
1 stalk celery, finely chopped
1 bay leaf
30 ml/2 tbsp Worcestershire sauce
120 ml/4 fl oz orange juice

OVEN TEMPERATURE: 180°C/350°F/Gas Mark 4

≈ Remove the neck and organs from cavity of the duck, and save for another use. Mix together the spices in a small bowl. Rub the duck inside and out with the spice mixture. Put the quartered onion in cavity, to draw any off-flavours, then put the duck on rack in a roasting tin, to allow fat to drain off.

≈ In a frying pan over medium heat, heat the oil. Sauté the chopped onion, garlic, celery and bay leaf until the vegetables are wilted, about 5 minutes. Add the Worcestershire sauce and orange juice, and heat just until mixture comes to the boil. Pour over the duck.

≈ Roast the duck at 180°C/350°F/Gas Mark 4 for 20 minutes per pound, basting occasionally with pan juices.

ROAST DUCK

CREOLE CHICKEN STEW WITH DUMPLINGS

This chicken stew in a spicy tomato sauce takes the better part of a day to make, but it makes a hearty dish that is worth the effort. It begins with a chicken stock, made with the chicken that eventually goes into the stew.

SERVES 4

CHICKEN STOCK

1 chicken, about 1.5 kg/3½ lbs, cut in half
900 g/2 lbs extra chicken necks and backs
2 carrots, unpeeled, cut into chunks
½ onion, cut into chunks
2 stalks celery, including leaves, sliced
1 bay leaf
7.5 ml/1½ tsp fresh thyme or 2.5 ml/½ tsp dried
4 black peppercorns
5 ml/1 tsp salt

≈ Put all ingredients into a large stockpot and cover with water. Bring to the boil and skim off the gray-brown foam. Reduce the heat and simmer for about 45 minutes. Remove the chicken halves and let cool briefly so you can handle them. Cut the meat from bones and refrigerate the meat. Return the bones and skin to the stock and continue simmering, uncovered, for a total of about 3 hours. Strain the stock, discarding the bones and vegetables. You will need 1.15 l/2 pts stock for the Creole stew; freeze or refrigerate any remaining stock for future use. Skim any fat from the top of the stock.

STEW

40 g/1½ oz lard
20 g/¾ oz plain flour
350 g/12 oz chopped onion
1 large green pepper, chopped
225 g/8 oz celery, chopped
2 medium tomatoes, seeded and chopped
1.15 l/2 pts chicken stock (above)
meat from 1 chicken, cut into strips or bite-sized pieces
1.5 ml/¼ tsp dry mustard
2.5 ml/½ tsp paprika
large pinch white pepper
large pinch cayenne
salt to taste
30 ml/2 tbsp chopped fresh parsley
dumplings (below)

≈ In a medium, heavy saucepan, make a red-brown roux of lard and flour (page 15). Remove from the heat and stir in the vegetables. Return to the heat and cook until the vegetables are limp, about 5 minutes.

≈ In a deep frying pan or large saucepan, bring the chicken stock to the boil. Add the roux and vegetables, 1 large spoonful at a time, whisking after each addition. Add the chicken and seasonings and simmer 30 minutes, uncovered.

≈ Meanwhile, prepare the dumplings.

DUMPLINGS

150 ml/5 oz plain flour
7.5 ml/1½ tsp baking powder
2.5 ml/½ tsp salt
5 ml/1 tsp dry mustard
1.5 ml/¼ tsp cayenne
2 eggs, lightly beaten
60 ml/2 fl oz milk
50 g/2 oz butter, melted
2–3 spring onions, finely chopped
30 ml/2 tbsp chopped fresh parsley

≈ Mix the flour, baking powder and seasonings in 1 bowl. Combine the eggs, milk and butter in a second bowl. Pour the liquids into the dry ingredients and stir just until blended. Stir in the spring onions and parsley.

≈ Drop spoonfuls of dough into the top of a steamer over simmering water. Cover and steam until the dumplings have risen slightly, about 7 minutes.

≈ Transfer the dumplings to the top of the stew and cook an additional 5 minutes, uncovered.

RABBIT STEW WITH LEEKS AND WILD MUSHROOMS

Wild mushrooms give this stew a heavenly accent. It is not a difficult dish. Start a day ahead by marinating the rabbit pieces, then use the marinade as part of the stewing liquid. The stew forms an excellent gravy.

SERVES 4

1.5 kg/3½ lbs rabbit, cut into 8 serving pieces
60 ml/2 fl oz olive oil
120 ml/4 fl oz dry white wine
2 sprigs fresh tarragon, bruised to release flavour
1 bay leaf
2 cloves garlic, finely chopped
2 carrots, peeled and sliced
1 leek, white part only, thinly sliced
dash of fresh-ground black pepper
60–120 g/4–8 fl oz flour
30 ml/2 tbsp olive oil
1 leek, white part only, thinly sliced
250 ml/8 fl oz dry white wine
475 ml/16 fl oz poultry stock (page 16)
40 g/1½ oz butter
225 g/8 oz wild mushrooms, any combination, quartered
hot noodles or cooked rice to serve

≈ In a glass or other non-reactive dish, make the marinade. Combine the olive oil, wine, tarragon, bay leaf, garlic, carrots, 1 leek and ground pepper. Marinate the rabbit for 24 hours in the refrigerator, turning and basting several times.

≈ Remove the rabbit and vegetables from marinade, and discard the bay leaf. Save the marinade. Finely chop the tarragon. Pat the rabbit pieces dry and dredge in flour.

≈ In a Dutch oven or large pot, heat 30 ml/2 tbsp olive oil. Brown the rabbit pieces on all sides, then remove. Sauté the vegetables from the marinade, along with 1 fresh chopped leek. Add the tarragon, rabbit pieces, wine and stock to the pot and bring to the boil. Reduce the heat and simmer 30 minutes, uncovered. Skim fat from surface.

≈ In a small frying pan, melt the butter. Sauté the mushrooms about 7 minutes. Add the mushrooms to the stew, and continue cooking until the rabbit is tender, about 30 minutes longer. Serve the stew over hot noodles or rice.

ROAST PORK WITH APPLE-WALNUT STUFFING

As elegant as it looks, this stuffed roast is not difficult to make. The most important tools are string to retie the roast after stuffing, a meat thermometer to determine when it is cooked through and a sharp carving knife. The stuffing is delicious – tart apples complemented by sautéed onions, the sweetness of sultanas, the crunch of walnuts, and just a touch of cloves for spiciness. You may want to make some extra stuffing to serve on the side. The walnut halves should be cut into 2-4 pieces each, but not chopped any smaller. If the sultanas are dry, soak in hot water for 20 minutes, then drain. You may substitute raisins, if necessary, but the sweetness is not the same.

The roast is easiest to handle if you buy it butterflied and still in one piece. But if the roast is cut in half, you can still stuff it and tie it back together, it's just a little messier.

SERVES 8

75 g/3 oz butter, divided
2 large Pippin or other tart apples, peeled, cored and cut into 1 cm/½-in. chunks
a small onion, chopped
2 stalks celery, chopped
1 clove garlic, finely chopped
175 g/6 oz soft breadcrumbs
100 g/4 oz walnut pieces
75 g/3 oz sultanas
2.5 ml/½ tsp salt
1.5 ml/¼ tsp ground cloves
2.5 ml/½ tsp dry mustard
1 boned pork loin roast, 1.5–1.6 kg/3–3½ lbs
30–45 ml/2–3 tbsp vegetable oil

OVEN TEMPERATURE: 190°C/375°F/Gas Mark 5

≈ In a medium frying pan, melt 40 g/1½ oz butter. Sauté the apples until barely tender, 7-10 minutes. Remove the apples, set aside.

≈ Add 40 g/1½ oz butter to the frying pan, and sauté the onions, celery and garlic until onions are limp, about 5 minutes. Set aside.

≈ In large bowl, combine the apples, sautéed vegetables, breadcrumbs, walnuts, sultanas, salt, cloves and dry mustard. This stuffing is not intended to adhere in a solid mass, but it should be moist. If the pan juices are not sufficient, add a little milk. Set the stuffing aside.

≈ If the pork has not already been butterflied, cut it almost in half along its length. Spread it out and make lengthways slashes along its thickest parts. If it is already cut in half, make 1 or 2 lengthways slashes in each half.

≈ In a large frying pan, heat the oil. Briefly cook the pork until the outside is browned, then remove from the pan. Set on a flat surface and spread it out with 4-6 lengths of kitchen string underneath. Mound the stuffing into the slashes. Carefully bring up the sides of the roast and tightly tie into a roll. If the stuffing falls out while you are reshaping the roast, just stuff it back in.

≈ Place the retied roast on a rack in a roasting tin. Cook at 190°C/375°F/Gas Mark 5 until a thermometer inserted in the thickest part of the meat (but not inserted so far that it is measuring the temperature of the stuffing rather than the meat) registers at least 65°C/150°F. This reading gives a very moist and slightly pink pork, and is hot enough to kill any trichinosis parasites. You may cook to 75°C/165°F if you prefer well-done pork. To estimate cooking time, figure 25-30 minutes per pound, but rely on the thermometer to tell you when it is done.

≈ Remove the roast from the oven and let it sit for 15 minutes before carving.

NOTE:

≈ If there is any leftover stuffing, or if you have made extra, put it in a lightly buttered casserole dish and cook for 15-25 minutes (depending on quantity) at 190°C/375°F/ Gas Mark 5.

PASTA AND RICE
MAIN DISHES

—★—

DUCK RICE

Use leftover duck meat for this delicious, one-dish meal. If you have only a few scraps of duck left, add them to the rice and use it as a side dish instead of a main dish.

SERVES 4-6

30 ml/2 tbsp duck fat or vegetable oil
100 g/4 oz chopped onions
50 g/2 oz sliced mushrooms
350 g/12 oz uncooked rice
750 ml/1¼ pts duck stock
10 ml/2 tsp salt
10 ml/2 tsp fresh thyme or 2.5 ml/½ tsp dried
10 ml/2 tsp paprika
2.5 ml/½ tsp black pepper
30 ml/2 tbsp finely chopped celery leaves
100 g/4 oz chopped spring onions
350 g/12 oz cooked duck meat, cut into strips or bite-size pieces

OVEN TEMPERATURE: 180°C/350°F/Gas Mark 4

≈ In a frying pan over medium heat, heat the duck fat or oil. Sauté the onions and mushrooms until the onions are translucent, about 5 minutes. Add the rice and cook until it is lightly browned, about 5 minutes.

≈ Meanwhile, in a saucepan, bring the duck stock, seasonings and celery leaves to the boil. Combine the rice and stock mixtures in a lightly greased 2 l/3½ pt casserole dish and stir in the duck and spring onions. Cover and bake at 180°C/350°F/Gas Mark 4 until all the liquids are absorbed and rice is cooked, about 1 hour.

DIRTY RICE

Dirty rice is a traditional Cajun dish served as an inexpensive main course or in smaller portions as a side dish. The taste of liver in dirty rice is subtle, and the gizzards give the dish an unexpectedly delicious, meaty taste. You may substitute the gizzard cooking water for part of the chicken stock, if it is rich. This recipe is baseline spicy – the Cajuns eat it hotter – so taste before serving and adjust seasonings accordingly.

SERVES 6 AS A SIDE DISH

225 g/8 oz chicken gizzards, or a combination of hearts and gizzards
30 ml/2 tbsp vegetable oil
1 onion, chopped
1 stalk celery, chopped
½ green pepper, chopped
3 cloves garlic, finely chopped
50 g/2 oz chicken livers, trimmed and chopped
50 g/2 oz ground pork (not sausage)
250 ml/8 fl oz chicken stock or tinned broth
1.5 ml/¼ tsp black pepper
1.5 ml/¼ tsp salt
1.5 ml/¼ tsp cayenne
2.5 ml/½ tsp dry mustard
2.5 ml/½ tsp ground cumin
225 g/8 oz cooked white rice
2 spring onions, chopped
30 ml/2 tbsp chopped fresh parsley

≈ Put the gizzards in a small saucepan, cover with water, and bring to the boil. Reduce the heat and simmer, uncovered, for 1 hour, adding extra water if necessary. Drain the gizzards and set aside until cool enough to chop.

≈ In a large saucepan over medium heat, heat the oil. Sauté the onions, celery, green pepper and garlic until the vegetables are limp, about 5 minutes. Add the livers and pork and cook, stirring, until meat is browned. Add the chopped gizzards, along with chicken stock and spices and continue cooking until the liquids are slightly reduced. Taste and adjust seasonings.

≈ If the rice was not cooked with salt, you will need to add more salt here. Add the rice, spring onions and parsley, and cook just until heated through, about 2 minutes.

RED BEANS AND RICE WITH TASSO AND ANDOUILLE

The use of two highly spiced meats mean this is a very spicy dish. You can substitute ham hocks for the Tasso, but increase the amount of cayenne and black pepper or the end result will be very mild. The addition of vegetables at the end add crunch to the texture.

MAKES 6-8 MAIN COURSE SERVINGS

450 g/1 lb dried kidney beans, picked over
30–60 ml/2–4 tbsp vegetable oil or bacon drippings
450 g/1 lb chopped onion
4 stalks celery, chopped
2½ green peppers, chopped
2 cloves garlic, finely chopped
225 g/8 oz Tasso, cubed
225 g/8 oz Andouille sausage, sliced
2 bay leaves
10 ml/2 tsp salt
10 ml/2 tsp ground cumin
5 ml/1 tsp dry mustard
15 ml/1 tbsp chopped fresh oregano or 1 tsp. dried
1.5 ml/¼ tsp black pepper
1.5 ml/¼ tsp cayenne
225 g/8 oz spring onion, chopped
1 stalk celery, chopped
½ green pepper, chopped
45 ml/3 tbsp chopped fresh parsley
575–675 kg/1¼–1½ lb cooked rice to serve

≈ In 4.5 l/1 gallon water, soak the beans at least 4 hours or overnight. Drain, rinse and return to the large pot with 1.25 l/2¼ pts water. Bring to the boil, then reduce the heat and simmer, skimming the foam, while you prepare the vegetables.

≈ In the meanwhile, in a frying pan, heat the oil or drippings and sauté the 450 g/1 lb onion, 4 chopped stalks celery, the chopped green peppers and 2 cloves garlic until wilted, about 5 minutes. Unless you use a very large frying pan, it is easier to sauté the vegetables in 2 batches. Add the vegetables to the beans, along with the Tasso, sausage and seasonings and continue simmering, stirring occasionally, until beans are tender, 1-1½ hours. Add extra water if necessary. Taste and adjust seasonings.

≈ Just before serving, stir in the last measure of spring onions, celery, green pepper and parsley and mix well. Serve over rice.

RED BEANS AND RICE WITH TASSO AND ANDOUILLE

MEATLESS RED BEANS AND RICE

MEATLESS RED BEANS AND RICE

Serve this flavourful, slow-cooked dish with salsa and soured cream. Extra vegetables are added near the end.

SERVES 6-8

450 g/1 lb dry kidney beans, picked over
45 ml/3 tbsp olive oil
1 large onion, chopped
4 garlic cloves, finely chopped
2 stalks celery, chopped
1 carrot, chopped
1 green pepper, seeded and chopped
15 ml/1 tbsp salt
1.5 ml/¼ tsp cayenne
1.5 ml/¼ tsp white pepper
1.5 ml/¼ tsp black pepper
5 ml/1 tsp dried thyme
7.5 ml/1½ tsp ground cumin
5 ml/1 tsp dry mustard
1 bay leaf
175 ml/6-oz tin tomato purée
120 ml/4 fl oz dry red wine
few drops of Tabasco sauce
1 stalk celery, chopped
½ green pepper, chopped
4 spring onions, chopped
450–575 g/1–1¼ lb cooked rice to serve
soured cream

SALSA

2 large tomatoes, seeded and chopped
4 spring onions, chopped
½ long mild chilli, such as Anaheim or poblano
15 ml/1 tbsp fresh chopped parsley
15 ml/1 tbsp white wine vinegar
15 ml/1 tbsp olive oil
few drops Tabasco, to taste

≈ In 4.5 l/1 gallon water, soak the beans at least 4 hours or overnight. Drain, rinse and return to the large pot with 1.25 l/2¼ pts water. Bring to the boil, then reduce the heat and simmer, skimming the foam, while you prepare the vegetables.

≈ In a frying pan, heat the oil and sauté the onion, garlic, 2 chopped stalks celery, carrot and 1 green pepper, chopped until wilted, about 5 minutes. Add the vegetables to the beans, along with the seasonings, tomato purée and wine and continue simmering, stirring occasionally.

≈ After about 30 minutes, taste the sauce, then add Tabasco to taste, and adjust the other seasonings. Cook the beans until tender, a total of 1-1½ hours.

≈ Meanwhile, in a bowl, combine all the salsa ingredients. Allow the flavours to blend for about 1 hour, then taste and add more Tabasco sauce if desired.

≈ Just before serving, stir the last chopped celery stalk, ½ green pepper and spring onions in to the bean mixture. Serve the beans on the rice, top with salsa and soured cream.

DUCK WITH PRAWNS AND FETTUCINE

Fresh herbs and prawns complement the duck flavour in this meaty sauce.

SERVES 6-8

30 ml/2 tbsp olive oil
4 garlic cloves, finely chopped
100 g/4 oz chopped onion
1 small green pepper, chopped
4 tomatoes, seeded and diced
225 g/8 oz sliced mushrooms
250 ml/8 fl oz tin tomato sauce
15 ml/1 tbsp fresh-squeezed lemon juice
30 ml/2 tbsp chopped fresh basil
7.5 ml/1½ tsp chopped fresh rosemary
5 ml/1 tsp paprika
1.5 ml/¼ tsp black pepper
5 ml/1 tsp salt
1.5 ml/¼ tsp cayenne
350 ml/12 fl oz duck or chicken stock
450–675 g/1–1½ lbs dry fettucine
475 g/16 oz cooked duck meat, cut into strips or bite-size pieces
225 g/8 oz medium prawns, shelled and deveined
6–8 spring onions, chopped
30 ml/2 tbsp chopped fresh parsley
Parmesan cheese

≈ In a large saucepan over medium heat, heat the oil. Sauté the garlic, onion and green pepper until limp, 5 minutes. Add the tomatoes, mushrooms, tomato sauce, lemon juice, seasonings and stock and simmer, 10 minutes.

≈ While the sauce is simmering, cook the fettucine in a large pot of boiling water. Drain and toss with a little olive oil to keep it from sticking.

≈ Add the duck to the sauce and simmer 5 minutes, uncovered. Add the prawns and cook until they are opaque and tightly curled, 2–3 minutes. Stir in the spring onions and parsley and serve over the fettucine, topped with Parmesan cheese.

PASTA PARTY

Crab-Stuffed Mushrooms
PAGE 26

Green salad

French bread

Fettucine With Veal and Artichokes
PAGE 82

Fettucine With Prawns and Andouille Sausage
PAGE 85

★

Praline Cheesecake
PAGES 110–111

FETTUCINE WITH VEAL AND ARTICHOKES

Use fresh artichokes for the fullest flavour, and fresh herbs because the sauce does not cook long enough to soften dried herbs. The result is a creamy, slightly spicy sauce.

SERVES 4

350 g/12 oz boneless veal, cut into 2- × ½-inch strips
5 ml/1 tsp salt
large pinch white pepper
large pinch cayenne
large pinch black pepper
1.5 ml/¼ tsp dry mustard
20 g/¾ oz plain flour
45 ml/3 tbsp olive oil
2 cloves garlic, finely chopped
100 g/4 oz sliced fresh mushrooms
4 spring onions, chopped
15 ml/1 tbsp chopped fresh basil
15 ml/1 tbsp chopped fresh oregano
10 ml/2 tsp fresh thyme
350 ml/12 fl oz single cream
1.5 ml/¼ tsp salt
2 artichoke hearts, cooked and sliced
2 spring onions, chopped
100–225 g/4–8 oz dry fettucine or other pasta, cooked

≈ In a small bowl, combine salt, peppers, mustard and 30 ml/2 tbsp flour. Toss the veal with the seasoning mix until all the veal is coated and all the seasoning is absorbed.

≈ In a frying pan over medium heat, heat the olive oil. Sauté the veal until it is browned, 6–8 minutes. Remove the meat from the frying pan and set aside.

≈ If needed, add another 15–30 ml/1–2 tbsp olive oil to the frying pan. Sauté the garlic, mushrooms, 4 spring onions, and fresh herbs until limp, about 5 minutes.

≈ In a small bowl or measuring cup, mix 15 ml/1 tbsp flour with 30 ml/2 tbsp cream until smooth, then stir in the remaining cream. Add the cream, salt and veal to the frying pan and stir well. Heat the sauce until it barely starts to bubble, then taste, and adjust the seasonings. Add sliced artichoke hearts and the remaining spring onions and cook just enough to heat through. Serve over the pasta.

CRAWFISH AND TASSO IN CREAM SAUCE OVER FETTUCINE

This quick-and-easy dish makes a rich, creamy, yet spicy sauce. It's also good made with large prawns instead of crawfish tails.

SERVES 4-6

75 g/3 oz butter
8–10 spring onions, chopped
3 cloves garlic, finely chopped
120 ml/4 fl oz dry white wine
120 ml/4 fl oz dry white wine
120 ml/4 fl oz seafood stock (page 17) or clam juice
150 g/5 oz diced Tasso
25 g/1 oz plain flour
225 g/8 oz cooked and shelled crawfish tails
475 ml/16 fl oz single cream
salt to taste
hot cooked fettucine to serve

≈ In a large frying pan, melt the butter. Sauté the spring onions and garlic about 2 minutes. Add wine, 60 ml/2 fl oz seafood stock and the Tasso and cook until bubbly. Reduce the heat and simmer until liquid is reduced slightly, about 10 minutes.

≈ Dissolve the flour in remaining 60 ml/2 fl oz seafood stock, then add to the sauce and stir until smooth. Stir in the crawfish tails and the single cream. Mix well and heat just until bubbly. Taste and adjust salt. Serve over fettucine.

PASTA

ITALIANS WERE AMONG THE ETHNIC GROUPS TO MIGRATE TO Louisiana during the 19th century, many of them from Sicily. Like every other group of settlers or traders, the Italians influenced the cuisine of Louisiana. Following are four distinctive dishes that combine pasta with crawfish, Andouille sausage and other prominent ingredients of Louisiana cooking.

≈ The recipes call for fettucine, but you can use almost any pasta, although some type of flat noodle is recommended. The measurements are for dry fettucine, but fresh pasta is even more delicious. Just remember that fresh pasta weighs more (roughly 50 percent more, although that figure varies widely) and you will need to increase the weight specified for dry pasta to arrive at the same cooked quantity. And it's fun to experiment with the different flavors of pasta that are available at gourmet stores.

≈ For 1 pound of pasta, bring 2 quarts of water to a boil. Add 1 tbsp. olive oil, 1 tbsp. salt and 1 crushed clove of garlic, then add the pasta. Boil, uncovered, tasting frequently until it is cooked to your taste.

≈ Drain the pasta in a collander, but don't rinse it. Toss it with a little olive oil to keep it from sticking. The pasta may be kept warm over simmering water.

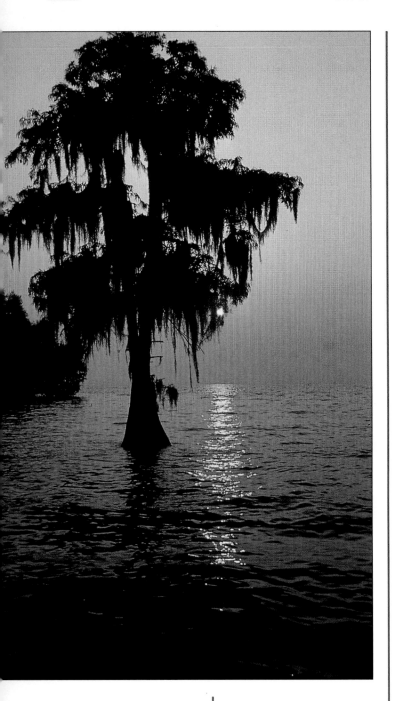

ABOVE A lone cypress tree rises from Lake Palourde against the setting sun.

RIGHT New Orleans has never needed an excuse for a parade or a celebration, but Mardi Gras is its biggest – a long, noisy and wild festival that brings people from all over the world to celebrate Fat Tuesday, the last day before Lent.

FETTUCINE WITH PRAWNS AND ANDOUILLE SAUSAGE

This is a moderately spicy dish, with the pepper flavour largely provided by the sausage, so be sure to taste and adjust the seasonings. This recipe uses a combination of fresh tomatoes and canned tomato sauce for speed, but you can substitute more fresh tomatoes for the sauce if you have the extra time to cook it down.

SERVES 4

30 ml/2 tbsp olive oil
2 tomatoes, seeded and chopped
225 g/8 oz onion, chopped
1 stalk celery, chopped
½ green pepper, chopped
15 ml/1 tbsp chopped fresh jalapeño pepper
2 cloves garlic, finely chopped
250 ml/8 fl oz tin tomato sauce
120 ml/4 fl oz seafood stock (page 17)
4 ml/¾ tsp salt
1.5 ml/¼ tsp black pepper
15 ml/1 tbsp chopped fresh basil
225 g/8 oz andouille sausage, sliced
cayenne (optional)
225 g/8 oz medium prawns, shelled and deveined
225–350 g/8–12 oz dry fettucine or other pasta

≈ In a large saucepan or deep frying pan, heat the olive oil. Sauté the tomatoes, onion, celery, green pepper, jalapeño and garlic until the vegetables are limp, about 5 minutes. Add the tomato sauce, seafood stock, salt, pepper, basil and sausage and cook until tomato and liquids are reduced, forming a thick, rich broth, 10-15 minutes. Tase and adjust seasonings. If you want it spicier, this is the time to add cayenne in large pinches, until you reach the right heat.

≈ While the sauce is simmering, cook the fettucine in a large pot of boiling water. Drain and toss with a little olive oil to keep it from sticking.

≈ Add the prawns to the sauce and cook just until they are opaque and tightly curled, 2-3 minutes. Serve the sauce over the fettucine.

VEGETABLES

—★—

CORN MAQUE CHOUX

There are many variations of this spicy corn dish, which can be made on the stovetop or in the oven. It's best made with fresh corn cut off the cob in your kitchen, but if you can't find fresh corn on the cob, use frozen corn kernels.

SERVES 3-4

25 g/1 oz butter
30 ml/2 tbsp vegetable oil
225 g/8 oz corn kernels (4–6 fresh ears)
½ onion, chopped
1 garlic clove, finely chopped
50 g/2 oz spring onion, chopped
15 ml/1 tbsp sugar
1.5 ml/¼ tsp black pepper
2.5 ml/½ tsp salt
1.5 ml/¼ tsp cayenne
120 ml/4 fl oz poultry stock (page 16) or canned chicken broth
15 ml/1 tbsp butter
1 egg, lightly beaten
120 ml/4 fl oz milk

≈ In a frying pan over medium heat, melt 15 ml/1 tbsp butter with the oil. Sauté the corn, onion, garlic and green pepper, stirring often, until the onion is limp and transparent, about 5 minutes. Add the seasonings, and stir until combined. Add the stock and reduce heat to very low and simmer until liquid has almost evaporated, stirring often. Stir in 15 ml/1 tbsp butter until melted and mixed in.

≈ In a small bowl, mix together the egg and milk, whisking until frothy. Add to the corn, stirring well, until the mixture is heated through.

PRAWN-STUFFED ARTICHOKES

Small prawns and Gruyère cheese make a delicious hot filling for artichokes. Serve these as a first course, or pour the filling over the top of toasted English muffins.

SERVES 6 AS AN APPETIZER OR 3 FOR A LUNCHEON

25 g/1 oz butter
85 g/3 oz sliced mushrooms
1 clove garlic, finely chopped
20 g/¾ oz plain flour
250 ml/8 fl oz seafood stock (page 17) or clam juice, divided
60 ml/2 fl oz dry white wine
dash of salt
dash of black pepper
dash of cayenne
30 ml/2 tbsp chopped fresh basil or 2.5 ml/½ tsp dried
225 g/8 oz small prawns, cooked and cleaned
50 g/2 oz grated Gruyère cheese
3 spring onions, chopped
6 artichoke hearts, cooked and trimmed
90 ml/6 tbsp grated Gruyère cheese

OVEN TEMPERATURE: 180°C/350°F/Gas Mark 4

≈ In a medium frying pan, melt the butter. Sauté the mushrooms and garlic 7-8 minutes.

≈ Dissolve the flour in 60 ml/2 fl oz stock. Stir in the remaining stock, then stir into the mushrooms. Add the wine and seasonings, and cook until the mixture is thick and bubbly. Stir in the prawns, cheese and spring onions, and cook over a low heat just until cheese is melted, about 2–3 minutes.

≈ Divide the prawn filling among the artichoke hearts. Top each with 15 ml/1 tbsp cheese. Place in baking dish and bake at 180°C/350°F/Gas Mark 4 until cheese topping is melted, about 10 minutes. Serve hot.

VARIATIONS:

≈ If you start with whole artichokes, add the tender part of the stem and leaf scrapings from 3 artichokes to the filling when you add the prawns. You may also stuff 4 whole cooked artichokes, with the chokes removed, and serve a dipping sauce on the side for the leaves.

RIGHT The explorer Jean Baptiste Le Moyne, Sieur de Bienville, saw in the swamps of Louisiana the vision of another Paris. He founded the city of New Orleans in 1718, with this riverfront square at the centre. Today Jackson Square is at the heart of the thriving Vieux Carre, or French Quarter.

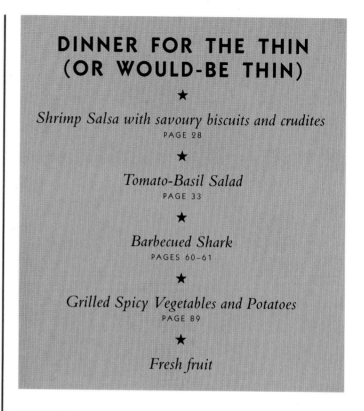

DINNER FOR THE THIN (OR WOULD-BE THIN)
★

Shrimp Salsa with savoury biscuits and crudites
PAGE 28

★

Tomato-Basil Salad
PAGE 33

★

Barbecued Shark
PAGES 60–61

★

Grilled Spicy Vegetables and Potatoes
PAGE 89

★

Fresh fruit

BARBECUED SPICY VEGETABLES AND POTATOES

Cooked with a minimum of fat, these grilled vegetables are an easy side dish when you're barbecuing meat or fish. Just arrange them around the edges of the grill.

sliced vegetables
olive oil
paprika and cumin or other spices
salt

≈ Slice red potatoes, courgettes or aubergines about 5 mm/ ¼ in thick or slightly thicker. Both these vegetables are attractive cut at a diagonal; cut marrow or gourds in half lengthways.

≈ Brush the cut edges lightly with olive oil and sprinkle with your favourite spices – paprika and cumin work well in this recipe, dried herbs do not. Lightly salt the potatoes, if desired.

≈ When the barbecue coals are no longer flaming, place the vegetables on the grill. Turn once during cooking: marrow and courgettes cook quickly, about 5 minutes; aubergines takes 1-2 minutes longer; potatoes take about 10 minutes. Cooking times are a little shorter if the vegetables are directly over the coals instead of around the edges.

GREENS AND TASSO

GREENS AND TASSO

Greens cooked with pork are a long-time staple of Southern cuisine. Here I use Tasso to give it a Louisiana twist. You can use chard, collards, kale, mustard or turnip greens, or a combination. Just remember that a huge pile of crisp greens will cook down to a very small mound.

SERVES 4

2 bunches greens
½ onion, chopped
75 g/3 oz Tasso, chopped

≈ Wash the greens very thoroughly, until all the sand is removed. This may take 3 or 4 washings. Tear the greens into pieces and chop the stems.
≈ Put the greens into a pot with the onion, Tasso and 1 cup water. Bring to the boil, then cover and reduce the heat and simmer, stirring occasionally, until stems are tender, about 40 minutes. Drain off water and serve.

PEPPERED POTATOES

Grilled or barbecued, these potato slices make a tasty side dish without the mess or large amounts of oil needed for French fries. They are very peppery, so beware!

SERVES 4

450 g/1 lb red potatoes, unpeeled, cut into ¼-in. slices
olive oil
10 ml/2 tsp salt
5 ml/1 tsp white pepper
2.5 ml/½ tsp black pepper
2.5 ml/½ tsp cayenne

≈ Brush both sides of the potato slices with a scant amount of olive oil. Combine the spices in a small bowl, then sprinkle on top of the sliced potatoes.
≈ Put the potato slices under a heated grill or on top of a barbecue grill and cook for 3-4 minutes. Turn over and cook another 3-4 minutes.

SPICY GREEN BEANS

Marinate these beans early in the day, and you'll have a spicy dish by dinner. These make an easy and convenient addition to a picnic or tailgate party.

SERVES 3-4

1 lb fresh green beans, topped and tailed
30 ml/2 tbsp vegetable oil
30 ml/2 tbsp white wine vinegar
15 ml/1 tbsp fresh-squeezed lemon juice
5 ml/1 tsp Creole mustard
1 garlic clove, finely chopped
1 spring onion, finely chopped
5 ml/1 tsp red-pepper flakes
1.5 ml/¼ tsp salt

≈ Cook the green beans in boiling water until just tender, 3-4 minutes. Drain and plunge into cold water, then drain well again.

≈ In glass or other non-reactive dish whisk together all the remaining ingredients. Add the beans and stir to coat thoroughly. Refrigerate at least 3 hours. Serve cold.

DEEP-FRIED AUBERGINE

Serve this spicy, crispy aubergine dish as an appetizer for those informal dinners when your guests are clustered in the kitchen, or as a side dish.

SERVES 5-6

50 g/2 oz Parmesan cheese, grated
75 g/3 oz cornmeal
5 ml/1 tsp cayenne
5 ml/1 tsp onion powder
5 ml/1 tsp celery salt
2.5 ml/½ tsp salt
2.5 ml/½ tsp garlic powder
2 eggs, lightly beaten
120 ml/4 fl oz milk
few drops of Tabasco sauce
1 large aubergine, cut into 5 mm/¼-in thick slices
vegetable oil for frying

≈ In a bowl, combine the cheese, cornmeal and spices. In a second bowl, combine the eggs, milk and Tabasco sauce.
≈ Dip the eggplant slices into the cornmeal mixture, then into egg mixture, then into the cornmeal a second time.
≈ In a deep frying pan or wok, heat 5–7.5 cm/2–3 in of oil to 180°C/350°F. With tongs, gently drop 3–5 slices of aubergine into the oil, taking care not to crowd, and fry until golden brown on both sides, turning once, about 2 minutes a side. Drain briefly on kitchen paper and keep warm in the oven as you fry the aubergine. Ensure the oil returns to 180°C/350°F before frying the next batch.

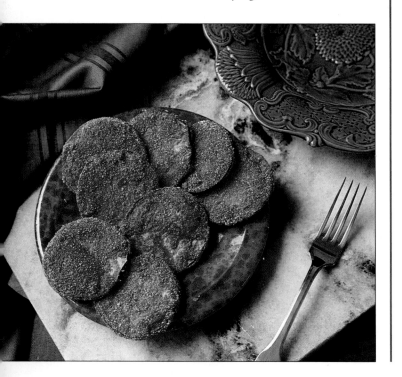

SCALLOPED POTATOES WITH TASSO

This is a Louisiana variation on a classic French dish, with Tasso ham and spring onions adding a Cajun flavour. You can use another type of ham, but you'll need to add extra seasoning that the Tasso provides here. This dish can be prepared in advance and refrigerated, with the seasoned cream poured over it just before it goes in the oven.

SERVES 6-8

1.25–1.5 kg/2½–3 lbs red potatoes
25 g/1 oz butter or vegetable oil
1 onion, thinly sliced
150 g/5 oz diced Tasso
8–10 spring onions, chopped
100 g/4 oz grated Cheddar cheese
100 g/4 oz grated Gruyère cheese
250–350 ml/8–12 fl oz double cream
5 ml/1 tsp paprika
5 ml/1 tsp dry mustard
2.5 ml/½ tsp salt
1.5 ml/¼ tsp black pepper

OVEN TEMPERATURE: 220°C/425°F/Gas Mark 7

≈ Leaving the skin on the potatoes, slice them thinly and place in a bowl of cold water.
≈ In a small frying pan, heat the butter or oil. Sauté the onion until lightly browned, 8-10 minutes.
≈ Drain the water off the potatoes and pat them dry with kitchen paper.
≈ In a large, ungreased casserole or baking tin (at least 23 cm/9 in square), put a single layer of potatoes. Follow with some of the sautéed onion, Tasso, spring onion and the cheeses. Continue layering until you've used up the ingredients, ending with the cheese.
≈ In a small saucepan, mix the cream with the seasonings and heat until just shy of a boil. Pour over the potatoes to a depth of 5 mm–1 cm/¼–½ in. Bake, uncovered, at 220°C/425°F/Gas Mark 7, basting with pan liquids once or twice, until potatoes are tender and most of the cream is absorbed, about 45 minutes.

SIDE DISHES

★

HUSHPUPPIES

Hushpuppies are traditionally paired with Fried Catfish (page 59), but they are a great side dish with any number of entrées, from Grilled Shark (pages 60–61) to fried chicken. You can use the same oil to fry hushpuppies and fish, but cook the hushpuppies first, then keep them warm in the oven.

MAKES ABOUT 20

175 g/6 oz cornmeal
50 g/2 oz cornflour
15 ml/1 tbsp baking powder
2.5 ml/½ tsp salt
2.5 ml/½ tsp garlic powder
1.5 ml/¼ tsp cayenne
1 egg, lightly beaten
250 ml/8 fl oz milk
25 g/1 oz butter
2–3 spring onions, finely chopped
vegetable oil for frying

≈ Combine the dry ingredients, then stir in the egg.

≈ In a medium saucepan, bring the milk and butter to the boil. Stir in the cornmeal mixture until smooth, then add the spring onions. Remove from the heat and let sit until it is cool enough to handle. Roll the mixture into balls the size of large walnuts or small plums.

≈ In a deep frying pan or wok, heat 7.5–10 cm/3–4 in of oil to 180°C/350°F. Drop the dough balls into the oil a few at a time, taking care not to crowd, and fry until golden brown, turning once, about 3 minutes a side. Remove from oil and keep warm in the oven while you fry the remaining hushpuppies. Make sure the oil returns to 180°C/350°F before frying the next batch.

CORNBREAD

CORNBREAD

This is a dense, moist cornbread, perfect for stuffings, such as for Crawfish Bisque (pages 43–45). It's also a good, basic cornbread to which you can add extras like grated cheese, chilli and corn kernels.

MAKES 9 SQUARES

40 g/1½ oz plain flour
175 g/6 oz cornmeal
4 ml/¾ tsp salt
5 ml/1 tsp sugar
15 ml/1 tbsp baking powder
2 eggs, lightly beaten
250 ml/8 fl oz milk
60 ml/2 fl oz melted butter

OVEN TEMPERATURE: 200°C/400°F/Gas Mark 6

≈ Lightly butter an 8-inch square baking pan, or spray with non-stick spray.
≈ In a medium bowl, combine all the dry ingredients. In a small bowl, mix together the eggs, milk and butter. Pour these into the flour mixture and stir by hand, making sure there are no lumps.
≈ Pour into the baking tin and bake at 200°C/400°F/Gas Mark 6 until a knife inserted into the cornbread comes out clean, 18–22 minutes. Cut into 9 squares.

OYSTER STUFFING

I like to buy extra chicken hearts and gizzards to give this stuffing a rich flavour. Use this to stuff a bird, or cook it as a stand–alone side dish.

SERVES 6–8 AS A SIDE DISH

heart and gizzard from bird to be stuffed (plus several extras if possible)
75 g/3 oz butter
350 g/12 oz onion, chopped
2 stalks celery, chopped
60 ml/4 tbsp chopped fresh parsley
15 ml/1 tbsp chopped fresh tarragon, or 1 tsp dried
5 ml/1 tsp salt
2.5 ml/½ tsp black pepper
175 g/6 oz stale bread cubes (preferably French, Italian or sourdough)
450 ml/¾ pt oysters, shucked, drained and cut into bite-sized pieces
1 egg, lightly beaten

OVEN TEMPERATURE: 180°C/350°F/Gas Mark 4

≈ In a saucepan, simmer the giblets in water to cover for 1 hour. Set aside and reserve the cooking water in case it is needed for moistening bread.

≈ In a frying pan over medium heat, melt the butter. Sauté the vegetables until limp, about 5 minutes. Add herbs, salt and pepper and remove from the heat. Chop the giblets and mix them in with the vegetables.
≈ Put the bread cubes in a greased 900 ml/1½ pt casserole dish. Add the vegetable-giblet mixture, oysters and the egg: the bread should be well-moistened but not mushy. If the egg and juices from the vegetables and the oysters do not moisten bread sufficiently, add the oyster liquor, or giblet cooking water, or milk.
≈ Bake, covered, at 180°C/350°F/Gas Mark 4 for 25 minutes, then bake an additional 5 minutes, uncovered.

BAKED CRAWFISH-CORNBREAD STUFFING

The tastes and textures of crawfish tails, sautéed mushrooms and toasted pecans set each other off nicely in this dish. Use it as a side dish with roast duck or poultry.

SERVES 6-8

100 g/4 oz pecan halves
25 g/1 oz butter
225 g/8 oz onion, chopped
2 stalks celery, chopped
1 medium green pepper, chopped
225 g/8 oz sliced mushrooms
30 ml/2 tbsp chopped fresh parsley
6 shelled crawfish tails, each cut into 2 or 3 pieces
5 ml/1 tsp salt
5 ml/1 tsp dried thyme
2.5 ml/½ tsp white pepper
2.5 ml/½ tsp dry mustard
1.5 ml/¼ tsp cayenne
1.5 ml/¼ tsp black pepper
170 g/6 oz crumbled cornbread (pages 96–97)
250–37 ml/8–12 fl oz seafood stock (page 17) or clam juice

OVEN TEMPERATURE: 180°C/350°F/Gas Mark 4

≈ Toast the pecans by spreading them in a single layer on a baking tray. Bake at 180°C/350°F/Gas Mark 4 until they appear slightly darker and drier, 10-15 miunutes. Set aside.
≈ In a medium frying pan, melt the butter. Sauté the vegetables and parsley until the vegetables are limp, about 5 minutes. Stir in the crawfish tails, pecans and the seasonings.
≈ Lightly butter or oil a 900 ml/1½ pt casserole dish. Mix together the cornbread crumbs, the vegetable-crawfish mixture and enough stock so the mixture is thoroughly moistened but not mushy. Spoon into the casserole and smooth the top. Bake at 180°C/350°F/Gas Mark 4 for 20 minutes.

TASSO BISCUITS

Serve this Cajun version of buttermilk biscuits piping hot with butter. Or, spread with mustard and add ham for tiny sandwiches.

MAKES 16–20 BISCUITS

225 g/8 oz plain flour
15 ml/1 tbsp baking powder
5 ml/1 tsp dry mustard
2.5 ml/½ tsp baking soda
10 ml/2 tsp sugar
2.5 ml/½ tsp salt
50 g/2 oz minced or ground Tasso
45 g/3 tbsp finely chopped spring onions
45 ml/3 tbsp butter
45 ml/3 tbsp lard
175 ml/6 fl oz buttermilk
double cream

OVEN TEMPERATURE: 200°C/400°F/Gas Mark 6

≈ In a large bowl, combine all the dry ingredients with the ham and onions. Using a pair of sharp knives or a pastry cutter, cut in the butter and lard until the flour is the consistency of breadcrumbs. Mix in the buttermilk.

≈ Roll out the dough 1-cm/½-in thick and cut into 5-cm/2-in circles. Put on an ungreased cooking sheet and brush tops with cream. Bake at 200°C/400°F/Gas Mark 6 until biscuits are risen and tops are just slightly browned, about 20 minutes.

TRINITY RICE WITH ALMONDS

Made with onions, peppers and celery – the Holy Trinity of Cajun cooking – this Louisiana version of rice pilaf has the added bonus of almonds.

MAKES 8 SIDE-DISH SERVINGS

25 g/1 oz butter or olive oil
1 stalk celery, chopped
1 small green pepper, chopped
100 g/4 oz onion, chopped
2 cloves garlic, finely chopped
75 g/3 oz blanched almonds, slivered or sliced
5 ml/1 tsp Worcestershire sauce
7.5 ml/1½ tsp salt
1.5 ml/¼ tsp black pepper
1 tomato, seeded and chopped
4–5 spring onions, chopped
30 ml/2 tbsp chopped fresh parsley
225 g/8 oz white rice

≈ In a medium frying pan, heat the butter or olive oil. Sauté the celery, green pepper, onion and garlic until limp, about 5 minutes. Remove the vegetables and set aside. If there is no oil left in pan, add about 15 ml/1 tbsp more. Add the almonds, and stir frequently until lightly browned. Add the Worcestershire and stir well. Set aside.

≈ In a large saucepan, bring 900 ml/1½ pts water to the boil. Add the salt, pepper, tomato, spring onion, parsley, sautéed vegetables and almonds and return to the boil. Add the rice, stir well and reduce the heat to very low, cover and cook until all the water is absorbed and rice is fluffy, 20-25 minutes. Or, to avoid scorching, you may turn off the burner and let rice cook in its own steam heat for the last few minutes.

SWEETS AND DESSERTS

———— ★ ————

BANANAS FOSTER

Quick and easy, this is a classic New Orleans dessert with a Caribbean flavour. If you double the recipe, use a large frying pan so you can flambé all the bananas at once; the liqueur does not flame as well the second time. For safety reasons, you'll need a long, fireplace-type match and a long-handled spoon.

SERVES 2

40 g/1½ oz butter
40 g/1½ oz brown sugar
2.5 g/½ tsp cinnamon
2 bananas, peeled, cut in half, then sliced lengthways
45 ml/3 tbsp brandy
45 ml/3 tbsp banana-flavoured liqueur
vanilla ice cream to serve

≈ Spoon the ice cream into dishes ahead of time.

≈ In a frying pan, melt the butter. Stir in the brown sugar and cinnamon, then add the bananas and sauté about 1½ minutes. Add the liqueurs and allow the mixture to heat for a moment – too short and it won't flame, too long and the alcohol will evaporate. Flame with a long match. With a long-handled spoon, spoon the flaming syrup over the bananas until the flame goes out.

≈ Put the bananas on top of ice cream, and spoon some of the syrup over the top. Serve immediately.

PRALINES

PRALINES

These chewy, buttery pralines are a rich New Orleans treat. Unlike many candies, where the nuts are added at the end, the pecans are cooked in the hot sugar and butter mixture to infuse the candy with the taste of pecans. This candy does not keep well.

MAKES ABOUT 24

225 g/8 oz butter
450 g/1 lb ted sugar
225 g/8 oz light brown sugar
120 ml/4 fl oz double cream
250 ml/8 fl oz milk
150 g/5 oz coarsely chopped pecans
225 g/8 oz pecan halves
30 ml/2 tbsp golden syrup
30 ml/2 tbsp vanilla essence

≈ Lightly butter 2 large baking trays, or line them with buttered grease proof paper or aluminium foil. You will need a sugar thermometer.

≈ In a large, heavy saucepan over low heat, melt the butter. As soon as the butter is melted, without allowing it to brown, stir in the sugars and cream. When sugar is dissolved and mixture is smooth, add the milk and chopped pecans and continue cooking a few minutes, until mixture is smooth and heated through. Stir in the pecan halves, golden syrup and vanilla essence.

≈ Cook over medium heat, stirring constantly, until mixture reaches 115°C/238°F on the sugar thermometer.

≈ Working quickly, spoon the mixture onto the baking trays. The mixture will be runny, but will set into patties. When they have cooled, remove them from the trays and wrap individually in foil or cling film. Store in an airtight container.

APPLE BREAD PUDDING

APPLE BREAD PUDDING

Using apples, this recipe is a variation on the traditional bread pudding with pecans and raisins, and is topped with a delicious hot cinnamon sauce.

SERVES 8

2 small, tart apples, peeled, cored and cut into 12-14 wedges
25 g/1 oz butter
30 ml/2 tbsp brown sugar
2.5 ml/½ tsp cinnamon
120 ml/4 fl oz milk
3 eggs
75 g/3 oz light brown sugar
75 g/3 oz caster sugar
5 ml/1 tsp vanilla essence
2.5 ml/½ tsp grated nutmeg
5 ml/1 tsp cinnamon
475 ml/16 fl oz milk
450 g/1 lb dry breadcubes (preferably French, Italian or sourdough)
sweetened whipped cream to serve

HOT CINNAMON SAUCE

50 g/2 oz butter
225 g/8 oz brown sugar
5 ml/1 tsp cinnamon
250 ml/8 fl oz single cream, warmed
30 ml/2 tbsp rum or 10 ml/2 tsp rum flavouring

OVEN TEMPERATURE: 150°C/300°F/Gas Mark 2
220°C/425°F/Gas Mark 7

≈ In a frying pan over medium heat, melt the butter. Sauté the apples, 5 minutes. Add 30 ml/2 tbsp brown sugar, 2.5 ml/½ tsp cinnamon and 120 ml/4 fl oz milk and simmer until apples are barely tender, 10-15 minutes. Set aside.

≈ In a large bowl, beat the eggs until frothy, about 2 minutes. Beat in the sugars, taking care that the brown sugar has no lumps. Add the vanilla, nutmeg, remaining cinnamon and milk, and mix well. Add the breadcubes and apples and mix by hand. Let the bread sit until liquids are absorbed, stirring occasionally, about 45 minutes.

≈ Lightly grease a 23 cm/9 in square baking pan. Turn the bread into the pan and bake at 150°C/300°F/Gas Mark 2 for 35 minutes, then increase temperature to 220°C/425°F/Gas Mark 7 and bake an additional 10 minutes, until the top is slightly crusty.

≈ For the sauce, heat the butter in a small saucepan until just melted. Stir in the sugar and cinnamon until smooth. Whisk in the cream and rum and heat until just shy of boiling.

≈ Cut the pudding into 8 pieces. Put hot cinnamon sauce into bowls with a piece of bread pudding on top.

BASIC PIECRUST

This recipe makes an 8-inch crust. For some recipes, such as Sweet-Potato and Pecan Pie (page 105), you'll want to bake the crust blind about 5 minutes before adding the filling. This will keep the crust from getting soggy.

100 g/4 oz plain flour
pinch of salt
40 g/1½ oz chilled butter
40 g/1½ oz chilled lard
15 ml/1 tbsp sugar
30–45 ml/2–3 tbsp ice water

OVEN TEMPERATURE: 200°C/400°F/Gas Mark 6

≈ In a bowl, mix together the flour, salt, butter and lard. Using a pastry cutter or a pair of sharp knives, cut in the shortening until the mixture has a coarse grain, with some bits of shortening the size of peas. Sprinkle the ice water over surface of the mixture, 15 ml/1 tbsp at a time, mixing with your hands until dough sticks together in a ball. You may also do this in a food processor, but use a very light touch or the dough will be tough. Mix in the last 15–30 ml/1–2 tbsp of water by hand so you can feel when it's ready.

≈ Wrap the dough in cling film and refrigerate for at least 1 hour, then remove from refrigerator 1 hour before shaping. Chilling makes the dough easier to handle.

≈ Roll out the dough on a lightly floured board with a floured rolling pin, until it is about 25 cm/10 in in diameter. Fold in quarters, place in a 20 cm/8 in pie pan, and unfold. Trim the crust to a 2.5 cm/1 in overhang. Roll up the overhang and pinch into a fluted edge.

≈ Bake at 200°C/400°F/Gas Mark 6, about 5 minutes for a partially cooked crust, or until lightly browned, about 12 minutes, for a completely cooked crust.

CHOCOLATE-PECAN PIE

It won't take a big piece of this chocolaty pie to satisfy a sweet tooth. Serve it at room temperature, topped with sweetened whipped cream.

SERVES 6–8

100 g/4 oz plain chocolate
50 g/2 oz unsalted butter
65 ml/2½ fl oz double cream
120 ml/4 fl oz golden syrup
45 ml/3 tbsp bourbon
2 eggs, separated
100 g/4 oz sugar
225 g/8 oz pecan halves
20 cm/8 in unbaked piecrust (see Basic Piecrust recipe on this page)

OVEN TEMPERATURE: 180°C/350°F/Gas Mark 4

≈ In the top of a double boiler, over hot – not boiling – water, melt the chocolate, butter and cream, stirring until smooth. Set aside and let cool, about 10 minutes.

≈ While the chocolate is cooling, mix the golden syrup and bourbon with the egg yolks. Gradually add about one-third of the chocolate to the eggs yolks, then add the yolks to the remaining chocolate and set aside.

≈ Beat the egg whites until soft peaks form, adding the sugar a little at a time. Gently fold the egg whites into the chocolate mixture until no streaks of white remain. Stir in the pecans, and pour filling into pie shell.

≈ Bake the pie at 180°C/350°F/Gas Mark 4 for 45–50 minutes. The filling will set, but will still leave some chocolate on a knife. As it cools, cracks may form in the top. That is normal.

VARIATION:

≈ Omit the bourbon, and add 15 ml/1 tbsp powdered instant coffee to the chocolate while it is melting, and add 5 ml/1 tsp vanilla essence to the egg yolks.

SWEET-POTATO AND PECAN PIE

Two Louisiana favourites are combined in this rich pie: a smooth, spicy sweet-potato filling and a sweet crunchy pecan topping. Serve this pie topped with sweetened whipped cream.

MAKES 1 PIE

20–23 cm/8–9 in pie shell, partially baked (page 104)

FILLING

75 ml/5 tbsp brown sugar, packed
45 ml/3 tbsp granulated sugar
22 ml/1½ tbsp unsalted butter
1 egg, lightly beaten
22 ml/1½ tbsp double cream
22 ml/1½ tbsp vanilla essence
1.5 ml/¼ tsp salt
4 ml/¾ tsp cinnamon
1.5 ml/¼ tsp ground allspice
1.5 ml/¼ tsp grated nutmeg
1.5 ml/¼ tsp ground ginger
350 g/12 oz sweet potato pulp (see Note below)

TOPPING

50 g/2 oz brown sugar
50 g/2 oz caster sugar
60 ml/2 fl oz golden syrup
1 egg
15 g/½ oz unsalted butter, melted
5 ml/1 tsp vanilla essence
pinch of salt
100 g/4 oz pecan halves

OVEN TEMPERATURE: 160°C/325°F/Gas Mark 3

≈ To make the filling, in a bowl, cream the sugars and butter together. When mixture is smooth, add the egg, cream, vanilla essence and seasonings and mix until smooth. Add the potato pulp and mix again until smooth.

≈ To make the topping, in a bowl, mix the sugars with the golden syrup until there are no lumps in the brown sugar. Beat in the egg, butter, vanilla essence and salt until the mixture is frothy, about 1 minute. Stir in the pecans.

≈ Pour the sweet-potato filling into the pie shell. Pour the pecan syrup over the top, spreading to make sure filling is completely covered. Bake at 160°C/325°F/Gas Mark 5 until a knife inserted in centre comes out clean, about 1¾ hours.

NOTE:

≈ You can use canned sweet potatoes, but make sure they aren't packed with syrup. Otherwise, bake your own sweet potatoes to make the pulp.

CHOCOLATE ESPRESSO CAKE

Serve this very rich and dense cake in small wedges. It cooks slowly, and will fall in the centre after you remove it from the oven. If that bothers you, fill the centre with whipped cream. Otherwise, use cream only as a garnish. Use only high-quality chocolate. The cake is best served at room temperature, so that the full flavor is not masked by the cold.

SERVES 12–16

450 g/1 lb plain chocolate
225 g/8 oz unsalted butter
20 ml/4 tsp powdered espresso
100 g/4 oz caster sugar
5 eggs
sweetened whipped cream
chocolate-covered espresso beans

OVEN TEMPERATURE: 120°C/250°F/Gas Mark ½

≈ Butter the bottom and sides of a 20-cm/8-in springform pan.

≈ In the top of a double boiler, over hot (not boiling) water, melt the chocolate and butter.

≈ Dissolve the espresso powder in 30 ml/2 tbsp boiling water and add to the melting chocolate. Stir frequently, until the mixture is smooth. Add the sugar and continue to cook until sugar is dissolved, about 5 minutes. (Be sure the water is not boiling or it may give chocolate a slightly scorched flavour.) Remove from the heat and let cool 10 minutes.

≈ In a large bowl, beat the eggs until frothy. Add a small amount of chocolate to the eggs, a spoonful at a time, incorporating the chocolate slowly so it does not cook the eggs. Mix the eggs with the remaining chocolate and stir well. Pour into the buttered pan. Bake until a pick inserted in the centre comes out clean, about 2 hours. Cool to room temperature.

≈ Just before serving, garnish with whipped cream and espresso beans.

RICE PUDDING

Rice pudding is a great way to use leftover rice. You may find yourself intentionally making too much rice for dinner, just so you have an excuse to make this old-fashioned custardy dessert.

SERVES 6

350 ml/12 fl oz milk
25 g/1 oz butter, melted
4 eggs, lightly beaten
75 g/3 oz sugar
5 ml/1 tsp vanilla essence
5 ml/1 tsp grated lemon peel
2.5 ml/½ tsp cinnamon
1.5 ml/¼ tsp grated nutmeg
75 g/3 oz raisins
225 g/8 oz cooked rice

OVEN TEMPERATURE: 160°C/325°F/Gas Mark 3

≈ In a large bowl, mix all the ingredients together, except the rice: spices have a tendency to clump, so use a wire whisk. Stir in the rice.

≈ Pour into a buttered casserole dish (this will come right to the top of a 1.25-l/2¼-pt dish) and bake, stirring once after about 15 minutes, until the custard sets, about 1 hour. Serve warm.

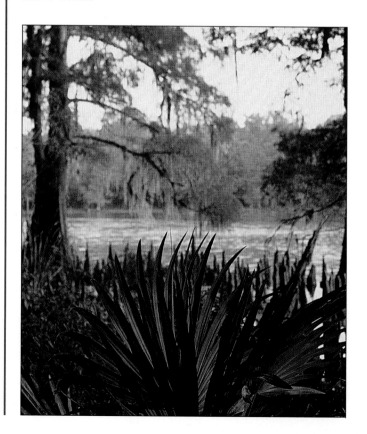

RIGHT A Palmetto cypress stands in the Louisiana bayou, the largest wetlands in North America. Brackish in the low salt marshes near the Gulf of Mexico and flowing with fresh water upstream, the bayou teems with seafood and game birds.

RICE PUDDING

LIME MOUSSE

A light, cool dessert, that is a perfect ending for a heavy and spicy Cajun dinner. The mousse showcases the taste of lime, so fresh lime juice is strongly recommended. Make this early in the day so it has time to set. It's most spectacular served in large stemmed wine glasses.

SERVES 6–8

1 package unflavoured gelatine
7 egg yolks
225 g/8 oz sugar
120 ml/4 fl oz fresh-squeezed lime juice
15 ml/1 tbsp finely grated lime peel
7 egg whites
150 ml/5 fl oz whipping cream

≈ In a small bowl, dissolve the gelatine in 45 ml/3 tbsp water. Set aside. If necessary to keep gelatine liquid, place bowl in shallow pan of hot water over very low heat.

≈ In a small bowl, beat the egg yolks until frothy, then add the sugar and beat until pale yellow. Add the lime juice and lime peel and put in top of double boiler over simmering water. Cook over low heat, stirring constantly, until mixture thickens slightly, about 10 minutes.

≈ Remove from the heat, stir in the gelatine, and set aside to cool.

≈ In a medium bowl, beat egg whites until they form soft peaks. Gradually fold the egg whites into yolk mixture together.

≈ In a medium bowl, beat the whipping cream until it forms soft peaks. Gradually fold the cream into the egg mixture until the mousse is smooth and no streaks remain.

≈ Pour into a large serving dish or individual dishes or stemware, and refrigerate at least 3 hours.

PEACH-AMARETTO ICE CREAM

What a delicious way to celebrate summer! This ice cream is made with a rich custard base and juicy, sweet, fresh peaches. Frozen ones will do in a pinch, but they are not as good. You'll need Amaretti, the light, crunchy Italian cookies made with egg whites and almond. You'll also need an ice-cream maker with a 1.75 l/3 pt capacity.

MAKES 1.75 L/3 PTS

350 ml/12 fl oz double cream
350 ml/12 fl oz whole milk
3 egg yolks
225 g/8 oz caster sugar
5 ml/1 tsp vanilla essence
1.75 kg/4 lb fresh peaches, peeled, stoned and chopped
15 ml/1 tbsp Amaretto liqueur or 5 ml/1 tsp almond extract
275 g/1 oz coarsley chopped Amaretti biscuits

≈ In a medium saucepan, bring the cream and milk to a boil. Remove from the heat, then let cool 10 minutes.

≈ In a small bowl, beat 3 egg yolks until frothy. Add the sugar and continue beating until the mixture is pale yellow. Add a few spoonfuls of the warm cream to the eggs, to raise their temperature gently without scrambling them. Add a few more spoonfuls of cream, then whisk the egg mixture into the rest of the cream. Cook over a medium heat, just until custard thickens slightly, but do not boil. Remove from heat and stir in the vanilla. Chill at least 30 minutes or for several hours.

≈ Meanwhile, purée the peeled peaches to make 475 ml/16 fl oz thick, chunky pulp. Add Amaretto or almond flavouring and let sit 1 hour or so.

≈ Put the cold custard and peach purée into an ice-cream maker. If your machine allows you to add ingredients easily later, wait until ice cream is partially churned before adding chopped Amaretti. Otherwise, add it now. Churn according to manufacturer's directions. Freeze until ready to serve.

LEFT A New Orleans establishment offers mint juleps, a traditional Southern drink usually made with bourbon, sugar syrup and fresh mint.

PEACH TART WITH RASPBERRY FILLING

This tart is luscious! With fresh peaches on top and a raspberry-cream cheese filling underneath, it's almost too beautiful to eat, but too delicious not to. Be sure to use fresh raspberries and peaches. The juices from frozen fruits make the filling runny and unattractive.

SERVES 8

FILLING

175 g/6 oz cream cheese
90 ml/6 tbsp soured cream
50 g/2 oz sugar
1 egg yolk
5 ml/1 tsp vanilla essence
5 ml/1 tsp lemon juice
75 g/3 oz fresh raspberries
4 fresh peaches, peeled and sliced
60 ml/2 fl oz apricot jam

TART SHELL

100 g/4 oz plain flour
25 g/1 oz sugar
pinch of salt
75 g/3 oz chilled butter
2.5 ml/½ tsp grated lemon peel
30–45 ml/2–3 tbsp ice water

OVEN TEMPERATURE: 190°C/375°F/Gas Mark 5

≈ Begin by making the tart crust. Mix all the ingredients except the water, in a food processor, or in a medium bowl, using pastry cutter or a pair of sharp knives to cut in the butter until the mixture has the consistency of corn-meal. If you're using a food processor, dump the dough into a bowl at this point. Add the water, 15 ml/1 tbsp at a time, and mix gently with your hands until dough sticks together: if you do this step in a food processor, you won't be able to feel when dough is properly moistened and will probably add too much water.

≈ Gather the dough into a ball, wrap with cling film, and refrigerate for at least 1 hour. Allow to sit at room temperature for another hour before rolling.

≈ Roll out the dough until it is 5–7.5 cm/2–3 in larger than a 23 cm/9 in tart pan. Put the dough into the tart pan, pressing into the edges, and cut off scraps, leaving a over-hang. Pinch the overhang into a fluted crust. Line with aluminium foil. Put pie weights or beans in the crust and bake at 190°C/375°F/Gas Mark 5 for 20 minutes. Remove

pie weights and bake an extra 10 minutes. Cool before filling.

≈ To make the filling, in a bowl, cream the cream cheese, soured cream and sugar with an electric mixer. Beat in the egg yolk, vanilla essence, lemon juice and raspberries, and beat until mixed. Pour into the cooled tart shell.

≈ Re-heat the oven to 190°C/375°F/Gas Mark 5. Arrange the peach slices on top. Melt the apricot jam and strain; spoon over the peaches. Bake at 190°C/375°F/Gas Mark 5 until filling is set, about 25 minutes.

PRALINE CHEESECAKE

This luscious dessert involves a number of time-consuming but not difficult steps. It's best made the night before or early in the morning it will be served. Your reward is a creamy filling with praline syrup swirled throughout and a tangy soured cream topping.

The pecans are the last things to go on the cheesecake, but should be made first to give the candy coating time to set. You will need a candy thermometer.

SERVES 12

SUGARED PECANS

50 g/2 oz caster sugar
50 g/2 oz light brown sugar
50 g/2 oz pecan halves

≈ In a small saucepan, mix the sugars and 45 ml/3 tbsp water. Bring to the boil, stirring constantly. Put the lid on and let cook 1 minute to let the sugar crystals wash down. Uncover, cook to soft ball stage, 110°C/230°F, stirring constantly. Add the pecans and stir until they all are coated evenly. Remove the pecans from the syrup and place on an ungreased baking sheet to set. As soon as the coating sets, move the pecans, otherwise they will stick to the baking sheet.

CRUMB CRUST

125 g digestive biscuits, crushed
50 g/2 oz ground pecans
50 g/2 oz brown sugar
75 ml/5 tbsp butter, melted

OVEN TEMPERATURE: 180°C/350°F/Gas Mark 4

≈ Mix all ingredients together: the crumbs will not form a solid mass. Press into the bottom and up sides of ungreased 23-cm/9-in springform tin: the side of the tin must be at least 6.5 cm/2½ in high, although the crust need not go all the way up. Bake 8 minutes. Let cool.

CHEESECAKE FILLING

275 g/10 oz caster sugar
675 g/1½ lbs cream cheese
225 g/8 oz ricotta cheese
10 ml/2 tsp fresh-squeezed lemon juice
5 ml/1 tsp vanilla essence
3 eggs

≈ Cream the sugar and cheeses together. Add the lemon juice and vanilla essence, mixing at medium speed until well blended. Beat in the eggs, 1 at a time, until the mixture is smooth. Set aside.

PRALINE SYRUP

50 g/2 oz butter
100 g/4 oz light brown sugar
60 ml/2 fl oz double cream
30 ml/2 tbsp golden syrup
25 g/1 oz finely chopped pecans
2.5 ml/½ tsp vanilla essence

≈ In a heavy, medium saucepan, melt the butter over low heat. As soon as the butter is melted, without letting it brown, add the sugar, cream and golden syrup. When the sugar is dissolved and the mixture is smooth, add the pecans. Cook over medium heat, stirring constantly, for 3 minutes. Remove from heat and stir in the vanilla essence.
≈ Pour one-third of the filling into the crust. Drizzle one-third of the syrup over the filling in a thin stream: you don't want to form a solid layer of syrup, but create a ripple effect. Add another third of the filling and drizzle more syrup over it. Repeat with remaining filling and syrup. Bake at 180°C/350°F/Gas Mark 4 until the top of cake is light gold, about 1 hour. Let the cake cool at room temperature, then remove outside the ring and refrigerate.

TOPPING

175 ml/6 fl oz soured cream
25 g/1 oz icing sugar
2.5 ml/½ tsp vanilla essence

≈ Whisk all the ingredients together. Spread over the top of the cooled cheesecake and garnish with sugared pecans.

BRUNCHES

—— ★ ——

BEIGNETS

Eat these doughnut-like treats hot with coffee, but watch for the powdered sugar that shakes onto your clothes.

MAKES ABOUT 30

120 ml/4 fl oz water, heated to 40–50°C/105–115°F
1 package (4 g/¼ oz) active dry yeast
10 ml/2 tsp sugar
175 ml/6 fl oz milk
2.5 ml/½ tsp vanilla essence
50 ml/2 fl oz melted unsalted butter
1 egg, lightly beaten
75 g/3 oz sugar
5 ml/1 tsp salt
2.5 ml/½ tsp grated nutmeg
425 g/15 oz plain flour
vegetable oil for frying
icing sugar

≈ In a small bowl, combine the warm water, yeast and 10 ml/2 tsp sugar. Let it stand until the yeast foams and forms a head on the water, about 10 minutes. If the yeast does not foam, the water may not be hot enough to activate it, or is too hot and has killed the yeast.

≈ While the yeast is proving, combine the milk, vanilla essence, butter, egg, 75 g/3 oz sugar, salt and nutmeg. Stir in the yeast mixture. Add the flour, 100 g/4 oz at a time.

After you have added 350 g/12 oz of flour, begin kneading with your hands. Add 15–30 ml/1–2 tbsp flour at a time, as needed, when all the previous flour is incorporated and the dough gets sticky. Knead until smooth and elastic, 8-10 minutes.

≈ Put the dough in an oiled bowl and turn the ball over a few times until it is coated. Cover with a towel and let stand in a warm place until dough is doubled in bulk, about 1½ hours.

≈ Punch down the dough. Roll out on a lightly covered surface to 1-cm/½-in thickness. Working at a diagonal, cut the dough into 5-cm/2-in strips. Then, at the opposite diagonal, cut the strips into diamonds. Put the beignets on an ungreased baking tray. Knead the dough scraps into a ball, then roll out and repeat process of cutting into diamonds until you have used all the dough. Cover the beignets with dishcloths, put in a warm place and let rise until doubled in bulk, about 1 hour.

≈ In a deep frying pan or wok, heat 7.5 cm/3 in oil to 185°C/365°F. (Remember that when oil gets above 180°C/350°F the temperature can shoot up rapidly.) Carefully put 4-5 beignets into the hot oil, making sure they don't touch each other. Fry until golden brown, turning once, 2-3 minutes a side. Remove, drain briefly, place on kitchen paper and keep warm in the oven while you fry the remaining beignets. Make sure the oil returns to 185°C/365°F before adding the next batch.

≈ Sprinkle the hot beignets with icing sugar, or put sugar in a bag with a few beignets at a time and shake.

BREAKFAST ARTICHOKES WITH CRAB

This very rich brunch dish begins with an artichoke base that is filled with crab meat, topped with a poached egg, and covered with a chive Hollandaise sauce. If artichokes aren't available, you can substitute halved English muffins. The artichoke bases should be cooked ahead of time. You may also make the crab filling in advance. The technique here is an easy way to make tempermental hollandaise sauce.

SERVES 6

25 g/1 oz butter
6-8 large fresh mushrooms, coarsely chopped
1 clove garlic, finely chopped
4 spring onions, chopped
pinch of cayenne
75–100 ml/5–7 tbsp double cream
225 g/8 oz fresh crab meat, picked over
15–30 ml/1–2 tbsp fine dry breadcrumbs
salt to taste
6 artichoke bottoms, cooked and trimmed
6 poached eggs

CHIVE-HOLLANDAISE SAUCE

4 egg yolks at room temperature
30 ml/2 tbsp fresh-squeezed lemon juice
15 ml/1 tbsp minced chives
2.5 ml/½ tsp salt
pinch of cayenne
175 g/6 oz unsalted butter

≈ In a medium frying pan, melt the butter. Sauté the mushrooms and garlic 3–4 minutes. Add 3 chopped spring onions and sauté 2 more minutes. Add the cayenne and 75 ml/5 tbsp cream and stir until well blended. Stir in the crab, remaining spring onion, and 15 ml/1 tbsp breadcrumbs. Add extra cream or breadcrumbs to moisten and bind as needed. Taste and add salt if necessary.

≈ Put all the sauce ingredients, except the butter, in a food processor but do not process yet. Melt the butter until it is bubbling but not browned. Process the yolk mixture for 3 seconds, then, while the processor is running, slowly pour in the hot butter until it is all incorporated and the sauce is pale yellow and slightly thick. The butter must be taken directly from the heat to the processor: if it is allowed to cool even slightly, the sauce will not thicken.

≈ Divide the crab mixture among 6 artichokes. Top each with a poached egg. Cover with Chive-Hollandaise Sauce.

CALAS

These sweet rice cakes are deep-fried, sprinkled with powdered icing sugar, and served for breakfast like small pastries. They are delicious hot, and it's hard to stop with just one or two.

MAKES ABOUT 20

2 eggs
75 ml/5 tbsp sugar
10 ml/2 tsp vanilla essence
2.5 ml/½ tsp grated nutmeg
2.5 ml/½ tsp grated lemon peel
2.5 ml/½ tsp salt
10 ml/2 tsp baking powder
225 g/8 oz cold cooked rice
100 g/4 oz plain flour
vegetable oil for frying
powdered icing sugar

≈ In a mixing bowl, combine the eggs and sugar and beat at high speed until pale yellow. Add the vanilla essence, nutmeg, lemon, salt, baking powder and rice, and stir until well mixed. Add enough flour, about 100 g/4 oz, to bind the ingredients.

≈ In a deep frying pan or wok heat 7.5 cm/3 in oil to 185°C/365°F. (Remember that when oil gets above 180°C/350°F, the temperature can shoot up rapidly.) Drop teaspoonfuls of the batter into the hot oil, but do not crowd. Fry until golden brown, turning once, about 4 minutes. Remove from oil, drain briefly, then place on kitchen paper and keep warm in the oven while you fry the remaining calas. Make sure the oil returns to 185°C/365°F before frying the next batch.

≈ Sift powdered icing sugar over the calas, or put the sugar in a bag, add a few calas at a time, and shake.

CALAS

SWEET-POTATO AND PECAN MUFFINS

These muffins are a delicious and less caloric – although not dietetic – alternative to other breakfast dishes like Beignets (page 113) and Pecan Crescent Rolls (page 117). Oat bran adds texture to the spicy dough. Bake your own sweet potato and purée the pulp, if necessary, or substitute canned pumpkin, but don't use sweet potatoes canned in heavy syrup.

I like big muffins, so I fill the cups to the brim with batter. To make more and smaller muffins, fill two-thirds full and reduce cooking time to 18–20 minutes.

MAKES 15–24

175 g/6 oz plain flour
75 g/3 oz wholewheat flour
75 ml/5 tbsp oat bran
6 ml/1¼ tsp baking powder
4 ml/¾ tsp baking soda
2.5 ml/½ tsp salt
275 g/10 oz light brown sugar
7.5 ml/1½ tsp ground cinnamon
4 ml/¾ tsp grated nutmeg
5 ml/1 tsp grated lemon peel
75 ml/5 tbsp vegetable oil
3 eggs, lightly beaten
350 g/12 oz sweet potato pulp
150 g/5 oz coarsely chopped pecans

OVEN TEMPERATURE: 200°C/400°F/Gas Mark 6

≈ Lightly grease 2 muffin tins.

≈ In a large bowl, mix all the dry ingredients together, including the lemon peel.

≈ In a small bowl, combine the oil, eggs, 175 ml/6 fl oz water and sweet potato pulp. Add to dry ingredients and mix by hand, stirring only until ingredients are well blended. Stir in the pecans.

≈ Spoon the batter into the prepared muffin tins. Bake at 200°C/400°F/Gas Mark 6 or until pick inserted in centre comes out clean, 24-27 minutes.

CORNMEAL MUSH

I remember eating perfectly-shaped rounds of fried mush when I was a little girl. My parents must have poured the warm mush into a tin can, let it cool, then cut off the bottom end and pushed the mush out so they could slice it in circles. This is not as pretty, but it tastes just as good formed in a loaf tin. Serve for breakfast with butter and maple syrup. Or, use the fried mush as a base, instead of rice, for gumbos and other rich-sauced dishes.

SERVES 6–8

5 ml/1 tsp salt
15 ml/1 tbsp sugar
50 g/2 oz butter
350 g/12 oz cornmeal
vegetable oil or bacon drippings for frying

≈ In medium saucepan, bring 1.15 l/2 pts water to a boil. Add the salt, sugar and butter, then gradually add the corn-meal, whisking to prevent lumps. Cook over medium heat, stirring constantly. Although the water will be absorbed and the mixture thickened in just a few minutes, cook for 10 minutes longer to get rid of the raw taste.

≈ Turn into an ungreased 24 × 14 cm/9½ × 5½-in loaf pan and chill until set, at least 1 hour.

≈ In a medium frying pan, heat the oil. Cut the mush in 1–2 cm/½- to ¾-in thick slices. Fry several slices at a time until golden brown and crispy, 6–8 minutes a side. Keep warm in the oven while frying the remaining slices.

PECAN CRESCENT ROLLS

These crescent rolls, made with a yeast dough and a sweet pecan filling, are irresistible served warm.

MAKES 24–32 ROLLS

DOUGH

1 package (4 g/¼ oz) active dry yeast
75 g/3 oz caster sugar
120 ml/4 fl oz water, heated to 40–50°C/105–115°F
2 eggs, lightly beaten
120 ml/4 fl oz double cream
75 ml/3 fl oz melted unsalted butter
5 ml/1 tsp salt
425 g/15 oz plain flour

FILLING

120 ml/4 fl oz melted unsalted butter
225 g/8 oz light brown sugar
20 ml/4 tsp cinnamon
100 g/4 oz pecans, finely chopped

OVEN TEMPERATURE: 190°C/375°F/Gas Mark 5

≈ To make dough, in a small bowl or measuring cup, combine the yeast, sugar and water. Let it stand until the yeast foams and forms a head, about 10 minutes. If the yeast does not foam, it won't rise. Make sure the water is the right temperature. If it's too cold, it won't activate the yeast, and if it's too hot, it will kill the yeast.

≈ While the yeast is proving, combine the eggs, cream, sugar, butter and salt. Stir in the yeast mixture. Add the flour, 100 g/4 oz at a time, and mix. After you have added 350 g/12 oz flour, begin kneading with your hands. Add 15–30 ml/1–2 tbsp of flour at a time, as needed, when all the previous flour is incorporated and the dough gets sticky. Knead until smooth and elastic, 8–10 minutes.

≈ Put the dough in an oiled bowl and turn by hand several times until it is coated. Cover with a dishcloth and stand in a warm place until doubled in bulk, about 1½ hours.

≈ Meanwhile, make the filling. Make a paste of the melted butter, sugar and cinnamon, then mix in the pecans.

≈ Punch down the dough and cut in half. Roll out each half into a circle about 38 c/m/15 in in diameter on a lightly floured surface. Cut each circle into 12-16 wedges, so it looks like a wheel with spokes.

≈ Spread half of filling on each circle, putting more toward the outside of the circle than in the middle. Beginning at the outside edge, roll up each wedge and turn ends in slightly so each roll resembles a crescent. Put the rolls on greased baking sheets, cover with clean dishcloths, and put in warm place to rise, about 1½ hours.

≈ Bake at 190°C/375°F/Gas Mark 5 for 12–15 minutes, watching carefully: the sugar that oozes out of the filling can burn easily, ruining the taste of the rolls.

CAJUN STRATA

Cajun Strata is the perfect way to serve traditional break-fast foods – eggs, sausage and bread – in an easy, one-dish package. Assemble it the day before and pop it in the oven one hour before eating. Serve it with fresh fruit.

SERVES 8

30 ml/2 tbsp vegetable oil
225 g/8 oz onion, chopped
225 g/8 oz mushrooms, sliced
2 garlic cloves, finely chopped
1 stalk celery, chopped
200 g/7 oz stale breadcubes (preferably French, Italian or sourdough)
450 g/1 lb Andouille sausage, sliced thin
350 g/12 oz Cheddar cheese, shredded
4–5 spring onions, chopped
4 eggs, lightly beaten
475 ml/6 fl oz milk
15 ml/1 tbsp Dijon-style mustard
5 ml/1 tsp salt
5 ml/1 tsp ground cumin
1.5 ml/¼ tsp black pepper
1.5 ml/¼ tsp cayenne

OVEN TEMPERATURE: 180°C/350°F/Gas Mark 4

≈ In a frying pan, melt the butter. Sauté the onion, mush-rooms, garlic and celery until limp, about 5 minutes. Set aside.

≈ Lightly oil a 23 × 33-cm/9 × 13-in baking dish, prefer-ably one that can be used as a serving dish. Spread half the bread cubes in the bottom, followed by half the sausage, half the cheese, half the vegetable mixture, and all the spring onions. Repeat the layers.

≈ In a small bowl, combine the eggs, milk, mustard and seasonings. Pour this mixture all over the top of strata. Cover and refrigerate overnight, allowing the bread to soak up the milk mixture.

≈ Bake, uncovered, 1 hour at 180°C/350°F/Gas Mark 4.

PORK GRILLADES AND GRITS

The thick, rich sauce soaks into the grits in this hearty breakfast dish to make a delicious combination. As an alternative, spoon the pork over rice and serve it for dinner. Either cook the grits following the directions on the package or as below.

SERVES 4-6

4 ml/¾ tsp salt
2.5 ml/½ tsp black pepper
2.5 ml/½ tsp cayenne
2.5 ml/½ tsp onion powder
2.5 ml/½ tsp garlic powder
2.5 ml/½ tsp dry mustard
1.5 ml/¼ tsp dried sage
450 g/1 lb boneless pork, cut into strips
30–45 ml/2–3 tbsp vegetable oil
100 g/4 oz lard
50 g/2 oz plain flour
100 g/4 oz onion, chopped
a stalk celery, chopped
small green pepper, chopped
1 clove garlic, minced
475 ml/16 fl oz beef stock
2 tomatoes, seeded and chopped

GRITS

5 ml/1 tsp salt
225 g/8 oz grits
45 ml/3 tbsp butter
1 egg, lightly beaten

≈ In a medium bowl, combine the seasonings. Toss with the pork strips until they are coated. Refrigerate several hours or overnight to let the meat absorb the flavours.

≈ In a medium frying pan over high heat, heat the oil. Add the meat and cook until lightly browned on all sides. Remove from the heat and set aside.

≈ In a large saucepan, make a red-brown roux of lard and flour (page 15). Remove from the heat and add the onion, celery, green pepper and garlic and stir until the roux stops darkening. Return to the heat and cook until vegetables are limp, about 5 minutes.

≈ In a separate pan, heat the beef stock to boiling, then gradually add to the roux, whisking after each addition. Add the tomatoes and pork and bring to the boil, then reduce heat and simmer 45 minutes, uncovered.

≈ Meanwhile, prepare the grits in a large saucepan. Bring 900 ml/1½ pts water to the boil. Add the salt and gradually stir in the grits, then reduce the heat and cook, stirring constantly, until all the water is absorbed and the grits have had time to lose their raw flavour, about 10 minutes. Stir in the butter and egg.

≈ Just before serving taste and adjust seasoning of the pork mixture. Ladle over the grits and serve.

SAUCES AND DRESSINGS

—★—

COCKTAIL SAUCE

TARTAR SAUCE

This tangy sauce uses bottled mayonnaise as a base, but if you are comfortable using raw eggs, begin with your own mayonnaise recipe and omit the olive oil and soured cream.

MAKES ABOUT 300 ML/½ PT

30 ml/2 tbsp olive oil
250 ml/8 fl oz mayonnaise
30 ml/2 tbsp soured cream
15 ml/1 tbsp fresh-squeezed lemon juice
50 g/2 oz chopped sweet-n'-sour pickles
15 ml/1 tbsp chopped capers
30 ml/2 tbsp finely chopped spring onion
1 clove garlic, finely chopped
2.5 ml/½ tsp salt
1.5 ml/¼ tsp black pepper

≈ In a small bowl, whisk the olive oil into mayonnaise, until it is incorporated. Whisk in the soured cream and then the remaining ingredients. Chill at least 2 hours to let the flavours blend.

COCKTAIL SAUCE

Prepare this tangy red sauce, with the sharp bite of horse-radish, several hours ahead and refrigerate so the flavours blend. Serve with Boiled Shrimp (page 65) or crab, or Deep-Fried Oysters (page 22).

MAKES ABOUT 300 ML/½ PT

120 ml/4 fl oz ketchup
120 ml/4 fl oz bottled chilli sauce
30 ml/2 tbsp prepared horseradish
15 ml/1 tbsp Dijon-style mustard
15 ml/1 tbsp fresh-squeezed lemon juice
15 ml/1 tbsp white wine vinegar
15 ml/1 tbsp Worcestershire sauce
2 spring onions, minced
1.5 ml/¼ tsp salt
1.5 ml/¼ tsp black pepper
few drops of Tabasco sauce, to taste

≈ In a medium bowl, combine all ingredients and whisk together. Refrigerate until ready to serve.

MUSTARD SAUCE

MUSTARD SAUCE

Here is a delicious and tangy alternative to red cocktail sauces to use as a dip for seafood.

MAKES ABOUT 300 ML/½ PT

250 ml/8 fl oz soured cream
45 ml/3 tbsp Dijon-style mustard
30 ml/2 tbsp mayonnaise
15 ml/1 tbsp chopped fresh dill or 5 ml/1 tsp dry dill weed
fresh-ground black pepper

≈ In a small bowl, whisk all the ingredients together. Chill for several hours to allow the flavours to blend.

VINAIGRETTE

This flavourful salad dressing is excellent on green salads and pasta salads. If you prefer, substitute whatever fresh herbs are available.

MAKES ABOUT 175 ML/6 FL OZ

120 ml/4 fl oz olive oil
30 ml/2 tbsp white wine vinegar
10 ml/2 tsp fresh-squeezed lemon juice
1 garlic clove, finely chopped
10 ml/2 tsp Dijon-style mustard
1 spring onion, finely chopped
1.5 ml/¼ tsp salt
large pinch black pepper
10 ml/2 tsp finely chopped fresh basil
5 ml/1 tsp finely chopped fresh oregano

≈ In a jar, combine all the ingredients and whisk or shake well. Refrigerate for several hours to let the flavours blend.

VINAIGRETTE

BUTTER SAUCE FOR FISH

This rich, creamy sauce is delicious with Crab-Stuffed Fish (page 62) or Grilled Shark (pages 60–61).

MAKES 4–6 SERVINGS

1 spring onion, finely chopped
30 ml/2 tbsp dry white wine
30 ml/2 tbsp white wine vinegar
50 g/2 oz butter
60 ml/2 fl oz double cream
salt
white pepper

≈ In a small saucepan, simmer the onion, wine and vinegar until the liquid is reduced to 15 ml/1 tbsp. Over very low heat, whisk in the butter, 15 ml/1 tbsp at a time. Whisk in the cream until smooth. Warm, but don't let sauce bubble. Season with salt and pepper to taste.

VARIATION:

≈ Add 15 ml/1 tbsp chopped fresh dill at the beginning, before the reduction. Add 15 ml/1 tbsp chopped fresh dill with the salt and pepper. This variation works particularly well with the Grilled Shark recipe (pages 60–61).

RÉMOULADE SAUCE

Traditionally this sauce is mixed with cold cooked prawns and served over lettuce with various garnishes such as tomatoes and olives, but it can also be used as a seafood dip. With recent health concerns about use of uncooked eggs, I based this sauce on bottled mayonnaise. If you're comfortable using raw eggs, begin with your own home-made mayonnaise recipe, and omit the olive oil and soured cream.

MAKES ABOUT 225 ML/8 FL OZ

15 ml/1 tbsp olive oil
120 ml/4 fl oz mayonnaise
30 ml/2 tbsp soured cream
1 hard-boiled egg, shelled and finely chopped
15 ml/1 tbsp capers, drained and chopped
1 clove garlic, squeezed through garlic press
15 ml/1 tbsp finely chopped fresh parsley
2 spring onions, finely chopped
30 ml/2 tbsp ketchup
5 ml/1 tsp lemon juice
15 ml/1 tbsp Creole mustard
2.5 ml/½ tsp prepared horseradish
1.5 ml/¼ tsp cayenne
1.5 ml/¼ tsp salt
few drops of Tabasco sauce

≈ In a medium bowl, whisk the olive oil into the mayonnaise until it is all absorbed. Add the remaining ingredients and whisk until smooth. Check the seasoning and adjust, then chill for several hours or overnight to let flavours blend.

INDEX